Jung Uncorked
Book One

Marie-Louise von Franz, Honorary Patron

**Studies in Jungian Psychology
by Jungian Analysts**

Daryl Sharp, General Editor

JUNG UNCORKED

Rare Vintages from the Cellar
of Analytical Psychology

BOOK ONE

Decanted with commentaries by
DARYL SHARP

For those in search of meaning

Sharp, Daryl, 1936-
  Jung Uncorked: rare vintages from the cellar of
  analytical psychology / Daryl Sharp.

  (Studies in Jungian psychology by Jungian analysts; 120, 121)

  Includes bibliographical references and index.

  ISBN 978-1-894574-21-1 (bk. 1)
  ISBN 978-1-894574-22-8 (bk. 2)

  1.   Jungian psychology. I. Title. II. Series.

  BF173.S517 2008   150.19'54   C2007-905580-X

INNER CITY BOOKS
Box 1271, Station Q, Toronto, ON M4T 2P4, Canada

Telephone (416) 927-0355 / Fax (416) 924-1814

Toll-free (Canada and U.S.): Tel 1-888-927-0355 / Fax 1-888-924-1814

Web site: www.innercitybooks.net
E-mail: booksales@innercitybooks.net

Honorary Patron: Marie-Louise von Franz.
Publisher and General Editor: Daryl Sharp.
Senior Editor: Victoria Cowan.
Office Manager: Scott Milligen.

INNER CITY BOOKS was founded in 1980 to promote the
understanding and practical application of the work of C.G. Jung.

Printed and bound in Canada by Thistle Printing Ltd.

CONTENTS

See final pages for descriptions of other titles in this Series

BOOK TWO *(published separately):*

See final pages for descriptions of other titles in this Series

But now the days are short,
I'm in the autumn of the year,
And now I think of my life
as vintage wine from fine old kegs.
From the brim to the dregs,
it pours sweet and clear,
It was a very good year.
—Frank Sinatra, *It Was a Very Good Year*

Life is short. If you don't wake up,
you might miss it.
—*Prof. Adam Brillig (ret.)*

Everything young grows old, all beauty fades, all heat cools, all
brightness dims, and every truth becomes stale and trite. . . .
A truth is valid in the end only if it suffers change and bears new
witness in new images, in new tongues, like a new wine that is put
into new bottles.
—*C.G. Jung, Symbols of Transformation.*

We need more psychology. We need more understanding
of human nature, because the only real danger that exists
is man himself. He is the great danger,
and we are pitifully unaware of it.

—C.G. Jung, "The 'Face to Face' Interview," 1959.

Preface

C.G. Jung died in 1961 at the age of 86, but his legacy lives on, mightily. His writings are like fine, full-bodied wines—they mature with age, as do we all if we pay sufficient attention to ourselves.

This book celebrates Jung. It presents spirited passages in his *Collected Works* (CW) together with my experiential commentaries on their psychological significance and contemporary relevance. The selections here are of course just the tip of the wine cellar, so to speak, that is Jung's legacy and, by extension, the backdrop to the attitude toward the psyche that generally informs the modern practice of analytical psychology.

Some of the material here may be familiar to readers from other contexts. That is to be expected and welcomed. Consider that we all come back to psychological writings anew, according to where we are on our spiral path of individuation and self-understanding. For myself, after thirty years practicing as a Jungian analyst, and editing and publishing books by many colleagues, I am still struck by Jung's all-encompassing wisdom and insights into the workings of the human psyche. Indeed, although I am quite familiar with the essays in Jung's *Collected Works,* wherever I open a volume it is as if I had never read it before. My knees become weak and I am inspirited anew.

In order to cover Jung's wide range of interests, the chapters here deal with one essay from each volume of the *Collected Works,* sequentially from CW 1 to CW 18.

For my and the reader's convenience, .*Jung Uncorked* is published in two volumes. Book One explicates and comments on extracts from CW volumes 1-9i. Book Two does the same with CW volumes 9ii to 18.

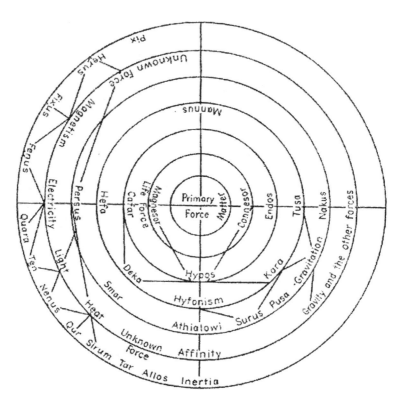

Figure 1. Helene Preiswerke's power mandala.

1

On the Psychology and Pathology of So-Called Occult Phenomena

(from *Psychiatric Studies,* CW 1; vintage 1902)

S.W. is of delicate build . . . face rather pale, eyes dark, with a peculiar penetrating look. She has had no serious illnesses. At school she passed for average, showed little interest, was inattentive. In general, her behaviour was rather reserved, but this would suddenly give place to the most exuberant joy and exaltation. Of mediocre intelligence, with no special gifts, neither musical nor fond of books, she prefers handwork or just sitting around day-dreaming.

At home and from friends she heard about table-turning and began to take an interest in it. She asked to be allowed to take part in such experiments, and her desire was soon gratified. . . . It was then discovered that she was an excellent medium. Communications of a serious nature arrived and were received amid general astonishment.[1]

As a young man on the brink of his career in psychiatry, Jung was already intrigued by the unknown. When he learned that his adolescent cousin, Helene Preiswerke (code name S.W. in the essay), had experienced bouts of somnabulism and auditory hallucinations, he agreed to take part in seances with her. Subsequently, encouraged by his mentor, the esteemed Eugene Bleuler (then head of the Burgholzli Psychiatric Clinic in Zurich), Jung presented his views on the case as his doctoral dissertation at the University of Basel.

This experience was Jung's first and only foray into the world of spiritism, but it arguably informed the rest of his life in that he was persuaded that there was more to our earthly existence than meets the eye. This fundamental realization was a seed that grew into his intense interest in alchemy and synchronicity—both concerned with

---

[1] CW 1, pars. 38f. (CW refers throughout to *The Collected Works of C.G. Jun)g*

the enigmatic relationship between mind and matter—and his life-long explorations of the instinctive source of mythology, religion and self-understanding.

The seances with Helene Preiswerke culminated in her production of a "power system," which under her direction Jung reproduced as a "round pattern" (figure 1, page 10) which only in later life, after much experience with similar patterns in mythology and dreams, did he recognize as a mandala, a traditional and widespread image of psychic containment and/or a striving for psychological wholeness. Thereafter, he often told those who came to him for help that they could help themselves by creating mandalas, which in fact Jung himself did when he was troubled (figure 2). The act of creating images in troubled times eventually contributed to his concept of the process of individuation, a fundamental idea in what we now call the school of analytical psychology.

Personally, I knew nothing of mandalas until I was on my knees. As elsewhere recounted, I woke up one morning from a dream and couldn't stop crying.[2] I found my way to a Jungian analyst who after a few months suggested that I draw or paint when I was in a mood. I tried that, but it didn't go anywhere because I was terrified by a blank piece of paper.

"Try this," said a friend who was also in analysis. "Take a page of a newspaper. It's not empty, not scary. Lay a plate on it. Draw an outline of the plate with a crayon or a colored pencil or a paint brush. Look at what you made and think about it. Now do something inside the circle. You can do anything you want— squiggles, faces, squares—anything. It's up to you; do whatever comes up."

I made some progress after that, and later read that Jung called such activities a form of active imagination, the object being to establish a line of communication between consciousness and the unconscious. It isn't necessary to interpret mandalas, to figure out what they "mean." It is enough to do them and live with them.

---

[2] See *The Survival Papers: Anatomy of a Midlife Crisis*, p. 52; also *Not the Big Sleep: On having fun, seriously*, pp. 107f.

Figure 2. Mandala by Jung.

Something goes on between you and what you create, and it does not have to be put into words to be effective. In fact, sometimes trying to articulate the meaning of a creation even interferes with that mysterious, personal dialogue between your ego and what's going on in the dark—the great down under.

Many years ago, after I separated from my family, I lived for a year in a basement apartment. It was tiny—a sitting room and a bathroom. It was pretty depressing and I cried a lot. But soon the walls were covered with my mandalas. I graduated from newspaper to cardboard to good quality bond. I used whatever drawing materials came to hand—pencils, pen, paint, felt-tipped markers, fingers. The images were crude depictions of whatever was going on in me when I did them. I didn't think of them as art, They had no style or technique and when I look at them now they seem quite grotesque. People who came to visit looked at me with suspicion. But I loved them and my soul (code name Rachel) rejoiced.

Such activities helped put me back on my feet. At the time I thought it was magic, and I still find their effect "magical," but now I consider such activity to be an effective tool in cooperating with the self-regulation of the psyche. It is serious play.

Active imagination can involve painting or music, dance or working in clay—whatever you feel like doing. You follow your energy where it wants to go. The less formal training you have in whatever you do, the better, for the trained mind inhibits freedom of expression. The aim of active imagination is to give the unconscious an outlet, so you don't explode with what's pent-up inside. It is also a way of establishing a container for your emotions—instead of dumping your moods on friends and loved ones, you keep them to yourself and take responsibility for what's yours.

Writing too is a form of active imagination. You can have a dialogue with your inner others about what's going on inside. You conjure up an image, personify it, give it a name and talk to it. You write it down to make it real, give it substance. That's the difference between active imagination and a daydream. If you don't fix it in time and space, it's pie in the sky.

In my case, once I started painting and drawing mandalas, I stopped feeling sorry for myself. I also stopped missing my family. I focused on myself and how I felt. Whenever I felt anxious and out of sorts, I captured the feeling with a concrete image or had a talk with my inner woman. I stopped imagining that my wife was responsible for my heartache; instead, I asked my heart why it ached.

I have often referred to my inner woman as "Rachel," but by any name she was and is my guide to a rich inner life and an understanding of my relationships with outer women. She doesn't always stop me from going off the deep end, but in general she's a loving life-line.

In the beginning Rachel was bound to the mother-mountain (figure 3). I sweet-talked her down, with a fierce determination to get to know her. (More of this later.)

Figure 3. The mountain-bound anima.

2
The Psychopathological Significance
of the Association Experiment
(from *Experimental Researches,* CW 2; vintage 1906)

We have been able to demonstrate fully this significant fact, the importance of which everyone psychologically oriented can easily gather, in hundreds of individual tests. It is, however, one of those not at all obvious facts that everyone doubts until he has convinced himself of its truth by conducting the experiment himself.

Thus we found . . . in my opinion the most important factor determining associations. We can see, from the fact that in the few seconds of the reaction we do not choose something fortuitous but unconsciously take an item from our memories, that our reactions, far from being the result of a free choice, are predetermined to the smallest detail by our complexes. The occurrences of everyday life are nothing but association experiments on a major scale: the things outside us are the stimulus-words to which we react according to what we are and have become, and never in any other way. No one can get out of his own skin.[3]

In the preface to this essay, Jung expresses his dismay over the lack of appreciation by his colleagues for his scientific research into the workings of the human mind, research that had been ongoing for several years before he made it public. He writes:

The relative youth of experimental psychology does mean that in this sphere little has as yet been clarified, and there is a great deal of controversy over many aspects of the subject. What is more, psychology is still a hybrid, inasmuch as the subject of experimental psychology is still in many institutions a very poor relation to philosophical psychology. The dogmatic nature of the latter is to blame

---

[3] "The Psychopathological Significance of the Association Experiment," *Experimental Researches,* CW 2, pars. 894f.

for the manifold misunderstandings between the two kinds of psychologist. One wants to make psychology a creed, the other a .science. Understandably these entirely divergent tendencies are in conflict with and hinder each other.[4]

Fast-forward a hundred years, and nowadays Jung's Word Association Experiment is seen as a landmark in the evolution of analytical psychology and our understanding of why we react as we do to what and who we meet in daily life, because it empirically verified the existence of complexes—those pesky autonomous personalities that often disturb us and our relationships.

Complexes are normal and present in everyone. They are the building blocks of the personality. Just as atoms and molecules are the invisible components of physical objects, so complexes are the hidden parts of ourselves. They comprise our identity and are what make us tick.

When I first went into analysis I knew nothing about complexes. I had heard the word, usually in a pejorative context, but I did not know what it meant. I had read about the Oedipus complex, which seemed to have something to do with a man's unconscious desire to kill his father so he could have his mother all to himself. And I had read about penis envy, deriving from a woman's supposed wish to sleep with her father. Well, that was Freud. It was rational enough, but it didn't explain the inexplicable.

Immersing myself in Jung, I learned that complexes are essentially feeling-toned ideas that over the years accumulate around certain images, for instance those of "mother," "father," "money," "power" and so on. I also learned that they have an archetypal core, which means that behind emotional associations with the personal mother, say, there is the archetype of the mother—an age-old collective image spanning the opposites, from nourishment and security (positive mother) to neglect and devouring possessiveness (negative mother).

---

[4] Ibid., par. 863.

The notion of archetypes was itself puzzling until I absorbed the following information:

> [Archetypes] are, indeed, an instinctive *trend,* as marked as the impulse of birds to build nests, or ants to form organized colonies.[5]

> Archetypes are systems of readiness for action, and at the same time images and emotions. They are inherited with the brain structure—indeed they are its psychic aspect.[6]

> It is not . . . a question of inherited *ideas* but of inherited *possibilities* of ideas. Nor are they individual acquisitions but, in the main, common to all, as can be seen from [their] universal occurrence.[7]

> Archetypes . . . present themselves *as ideas and images,* like everything else that becomes a content of consciousness.[8]

Jung used the simile of the spectrum to illustrate the difference between instinct and the archetype as an "instinctual image":

> The dynamism of instinct is lodged as it were in the infra-red part of the spectrum, whereas the instinctual image lies in the ultra-violet part. . . . The realization and assimilation of instinct never take place at the red end, i.e., by absorption into the instinctual sphere, but only through integration of the image which signifies and at the same time evokes the instinct.[9]

INSTINCTS	ARCHETYPES
infrared ———————————————————— ultraviolet	
(**Physiological:** body symptoms, instinctual perceptions, etc.)	(**Psychological:** spirit, dreams, conceptions, images, fantasies, etc.)

---

[5] "Approaching the Unconscious," in Carl G. Jung and Marie-Louise von Franz, eds., *Man and His Symbols,* p. 69.

[6] "Mind and Earth," *Civiliaztion in Transition,* CW 10, par. 53.

[7] "Concerning the Archetypes and the Anima Concept," *The Archetypes and the Collective Unconscious,* CW 9i, par. 136.

[8] "On the Nature of the Psyche," *The Structure and Dynamics of the Psyche,* CW 8, par. 435.

[9] Ibid., par. 414.

So, an archetype is a primordial, structural element of the human psyche, an instinctive, universal tendency to form certain ideas and images and to behave in certain ways. I could follow that. However, I still did not connect complexes with my own life and what they had to do with me finding myself on my knees. Then I did Jung's Word Association Experiment, the "test" he developed to illustrate how unconscious factors can disturb the workings of consciousness.

In this test there is a list of a hundred words (figure 4, next page), to each of which you are asked to respond with what first comes into your mind. The delay in responding (the response time) is measured with a stop watch, as for instance:

> "Head"— "bed" (0.8 sec.)
> "Marry"— "together" (1.7 sec.)
> "Woman"— "friend" (2 sec.)
> "Home"—(long pause) "none" (5.6 sec.)

—and so on.

Then you are put through the list a second time, and different responses to the same words are noted. Finally you are asked for comments on those words to which you had a longer-than-average response time, a merely mechanical response or a different association on the second run-through; all these had been flagged by the questioner as "complex indicators." With such information, a profile of your psychology can be compiled with great accuracy.

It was an illuminating experience. It was also deflating. It convinced me that complexes were not only real but were alive in me and quite autonomous, independent of my will. I realized they could affect my memory, my thoughts, my moods, my behavior. I was not free to be me—there *was* no "me"—when I was in the grip of a complex.

Freud described dreams as the *via regia* to the unconscious; Jung showed that the royal road to the unconscious is rather the complex, the architect of both dreams and symptoms. In fact, Jung initially gave the name "complex psychology" to his school of thought, to distinguish it from Freud's school of psychoanalysis.

		25. go	51. frog	
		26. blue	52. try	
1. head		27. lamp	53. hunger	77. cow
2. green		28. carry	54. white	78. name
3. water		29. bread	55. child	79. luck
4. sing		30. rich	56. speak	80. say
5. dead		31. tree	57. pencil	81. table
6. long		32. jump	58. sad	82. naughty
7. ship		33. pity	59. plum	83. brother
8. make		34. yellow	60. marry	84. afraid
9. woman		35. street	61. home	85. love
10. friendly		36. bury	62. nasty	86. chair
11. bake		37. salt	63. glass	87. worry
12. ask		38. new	64. fight	88. kiss~
13. cold		39. habit	65. wool	89. bride
14. stalk		40. pray	66. big	90. clean
15. dance		41. money	67. carrot	91. bag
16. village		42. silly	68. give	92. choice
17. pond		43. book	69. doctor	93. bed
18. sick		44. despise	70. frosty	94. pleased
19. pride		45. finger	71. flower	95. happy
20. bring		46. jolly	72. beat	96. shut
21. ink		47. bird	73. box	97. wound
22. angry		48. walk	74. old	98. evil
23. needle		49. paper	75. family	99. door
24. swim		50. wicked	76. wait	100. insult

Figure 4. List of Association Experiment stimulus words.

The activation of a complex is always marked by the presence of some strong emotion, be it love, hate, rage, sadness, joy, or simply irritation. Everyone is complexed by something, which is to say, we all react emotionally when the right buttons are pushed. Or, to put it another way, an emotional reaction *means* that a complex has been activated. When we are emotional we can't think straight and hardly know how we feel. We speak and act out of the complex, and when it has run its course we wonder what took over.

The existence of complexes explained a good deal of my occasionally aberrant behavior, feelings and moods. Oh, so that's why I fell in love with the hat-check girl. Oh, so that's why I dumped a bowl of salad on the head of the lady babbling to me at a banquet. And that's why I swore at the guy who cut me off on the highway. I was complexed!

We cannot get rid of our complexes because they are deeply rooted in our personal history. Complexes are the main fixtures in our psychic house. We can't get rid of them because they are part and parcel of who we are. The most we can do is become aware of how we are influenced by them and how they interfere with our conscious intentions. As long as we are unconscious of our complexes, we are prone to being overwhelmed or driven by them. When we understand them, they do not disappear but over time their grip may loosen.

Life would be very dull without complexes. They are the very stuff of history and drama, comedy, tragedy, films, novels and television sitcoms. Collectively they are at the root of wars between nations and religious conflict. On the personal level they can either spice our relationships with love and affection, or poison them with resentment, annoyance, self-pity, anxiety, fear and guilt. In short, a complex is a loose cannon, the elephant in any room with more than one person in it, a phenomenon widely experienced at family gatherings.

A complex is a bundle of associations, sometimes painful, sometimes joyful, always accompanied by affect. It has energy and a life of its own. It can upset digestion, breathing and the rate at which the heart beats. It behaves like a partial personality. When you want to say or do something and a complex interferes, you find yourself saying or doing something quite different from what you intended. Your best intentions are upset, exactly as if you had been interfered with by another person.

In some conditions, schizophrenia for example, complexes emancipate themselves from conscious control to such an extent that they can become visible and audible. They appear as visions and speak in voices that are like those of definite people. (Think of the Nobel-prize winning physicist in the popular book and film, *A Beautiful Mind*). But this is not in itself pathological. Complexes are regularly personified in dreams, and one can train oneself so they become visible or audible also in a waking condition. It is even psychologically healthy to do so, for when you give them a voice, a face, a personality (like my Rachel), they are less likely to take over when you're not looking.

We like to think we are masters in our own house, but clearly we are not. We are renters at best. Psychologically we live in a boarding house of saints and knaves, nobles and villains, run by a landlord who for all we know is indifferent to the lot. We fancy we can do what we want, but when it comes to a showdown our will is hampered by fellow boarders with a mind of their own.

Now isn't that typical. Just when you think you're in charge, you're reminded again that you're not. There are those who say you can overcome your complexes, but the best I've been able to do is to identify a few and know when they're active. Nor does this always stop me from falling prey to them. And that's life.

To sum up: complexes have a tendency to live their own lives in spite of our conscious intentions. Both our personal unconscious and the collective unconscious consist of an unknown number of these fragmentary personalities. This actually explains a lot that is otherwise quite puzzling, like the fact that one is able to dramatize mental contents. When someone creates a character on the stage or in a poem or novel, for instance, it is not simply a product of that person's imagination. Writers may deny that their work has a personal psychological meaning, but in fact you can read their minds when you study the characters they create.

The esteemed Zurich analyst Marie-Louise von Franz once told me of a man who after two years of bringing his dreams for analysis confessed to her that he had made them all up.

"The joke's on you," she told him. "Where do you think your made-up stories came from? You said what was in you. That's as real as any dream."

Jung saw complexes as islands of consciousness split off from the ego-mainland. This is a useful metaphor. When you're emotional, caught in a complex, you're cut off from rational ego resources; the complex rules the personality for as long as you stay on the island. When the storm dies down you swim ashore and lick your wounds, wondering what on earth got into you.

Jung was also wise enough to know that his own complexes were behind his psychological views. He did not denigrate the ideas of others such as Freud and Adler, but he did question why they did not acknowledge that their personal psychology played a major role in their theories.

"Psychology," says Jung (I am paraphrasing here), "is a point of view and no one theory explains everything. Whatever we believe has its source in our own history and our own complexes. I assume that those who are attracted to my views have a psychology similar to mine, and those who accept Freud have a psychology similar to his. So be it. I am not a tyrant. Let people believe what suits them. I don't lose any sleep over that."

And nor do I, for reading Jung stimulates me to think, question, doubt, and thereby helps me to understand myself better. And that—me, myself—is just about all I have to offer those who seek me out for a personal analytic dialogue.

"Seek not a cure," I sometimes say, "but a new perspective on what ails you." Dreams are a big help in this endeavor, for they have no axe to grind except to compensate the conscious attitude.

Because the Word Association Experiment is the most effective way to demonstrate the existence of autonomous complexes, having it done on oneself, and conducting it on others, have always been requirements in the training of Jungian analysts.

The inescapable bottom line here is that no one is so conscious that he or she cannot be blind-sided by their complexes, over and over and over again. Hence Jung cautions:

> Everyone knows nowadays that people "have complexes." What is not so well known, though far more important theoretically, is that complexes can *have us.*[10]

---

[10] "A Review of the Complex Theory," *The Structure and Dynamics of the Psyche,* CW 8, pa. 200.

3
On the Importance of the Unconscious
In Psychopathology

(from *The Psychogenesis of Mental Disease,* CW 3;
vintage 1914)

The unconscious contains all those psychic events which do not possess sufficient intensity of functioning to cross the threshold dividing the conscious from the unconscious. They remain, in effect, below the surface of consciousness, and flit by in subliminal form.

In normal people the principal function of the unconscious is to effect a compensation and to produce a balance. All extreme conscious tendencies are softened and toned down through a counter-impulse in the unconscious. This compensating agency .expresses itself in certain unconscious, apparently inconsistent activities.[11]

The discovery of the unconscious is perhaps the most significant event in the age-old pursuit of self-knowledge.

The existence of something other than our worldly ego concerns has been divined for eons. We now call this an awareness of the transcendental realm, aptly pictured in a nineteenth-century woodcut of a spiritual pilgrim glimpsing eternity (figure 5, next page)—but not until Freud and Jung came on the scene in the early twentieth century did the concept of the unconscious take hold of the popular imagination. Now there is no counting how many millions of hours people have spent delving into their nether regions in the pursuit of knowing themselves.

But still, most people confuse self-knowledge with knowledge of their conscious ego-personalities. Those with any ego-consciousness at all take it for granted that they know themselves. This is natural and widespread, thanks to René Descartes' famous dictum,

---

[11] CW 3, pars 439, 449.

Figure 5. The hole open to eternity—
the spiritual pilgrim discovers another world.

"I think, therefore I am."[12] But Descartes only knew the half of it, for the real psychic facts are for the most part hidden. The ego knows only its own contents, which are largely dependent on social factors. Now we know that without some knowledge of the unconscious and its contents one cannot claim to know oneself.

The average person knows little about the intricate physiological and anatomical structure of the body, yet we are accustomed to taking steps against physical infection. Complexes are just as real, and just as invisible, as germs. Against pervasive unconsciousness we are virtually defenseless, open to all manner of influences and psychic infections. We embrace dictators; we go to war; we believe what we are told. We can guard against the risk of psychic infection only when we know what is attacking us, and how, where and when the attack might come.

Self-knowledge is a matter of getting to know your own individual facts. Theories are of little help, notes Jung:

> The more a theory lays claim to universal validity, the less capable it is of doing justice to the individual facts. Any theory based on [experimentation] is necessarily *statistical;* it formulates an *ideal average* which abolishes all exceptions at either end of the scale and replaces them by an abstract mean. This mean is quite valid, though it need not necessarily occur in reality. . . . The exceptions at either extreme, though equally factual, do not appear in the final result at all, since they cancel each other out.[13]

Similarly, in the treatment of psychic suffering, Jung always stressed that the so-called scientific knowledge of humankind in general must take second place to what is ailing the particular person. On the one hand the analyst is equipped with statistical truths, and on the other is faced with someone who requires individual un-

---

[12] This is what is known in the science of logic as a *tautology*—"needless repetition of the same sense in different words; redundancy." *(American Heritage Dictionary)* So Descartes might just as well have said, "I think, therefore I think I am,"—and with as little insight. And why not: "I feel, therefore I am"?

[13] "The Undiscovered Self," *Civilization in Transition,* CW 10, par. 493.

derstanding. One need not deny the validity of statistics, but the more schematic the treatment, the more resistances it calls up in the patient. The analyst therefore needs to have a kind of two-way thinking: doing one thing while not losing sight of the other. One might say that analysts have to be two-faced, like the god Janus of antiquity.[14]

The recognition that there is an unconscious side of ourselves has fundamentally altered the pursuit of self-knowledge. It is apparent now that we are twofold beings: we have a conscious side we more or less know, and an unconscious side of which we know little but which in all likelihood is no secret to others and influences us in many ways we are not aware of. When we lack knowledge of that other side, we can do the most terrible things without calling ourselves to account and without ever suspecting what we're doing. Thus we may be baffled by how others react to us. The increased self-knowledge that comes about through depth psychology allows us both to remedy our own failings and to become more understanding and tolerant of others. A case in point is the typological differences between people, addressed here in later hapters.

Self-knowledge can have a healing effect on ourselves and our environment, but this seldom happens without a prolonged period of professional analysis. Self-analysis can work to the extent that we are alert to the effects of our behavior and are willing to learn from them; however, it is limited by our blind-spots—our complexes—and by the silence of others who for one reason or another indulge them. To really get a handle on ourselves we need an honest, objective mirror. Our intimates are rarely that. The unconscious is a rather more unsparing mirror, and analysts are trained to interpret the reflections. That is why the analytic dialogue is helpful.

Historically, the triad of repentance, confession and purification

---

[14] Janus was known to the Greeks as the porter of heaven. "He opens the year, the first month being named after him. He is the guardian of gates, on which account he is commonly represented with two heads, because every door looks two ways." (Thomas Bulfinch, *Bulfinch's Mythology: The Age of Fable*, p. 11)

from sin have been the conditions of salvation. That has traditionally been the province of religion: *extra ecclesiam nulla salus* ("no salvation outside the Church") and for some it still is, but among unbelievers—that is, those who are no longer contained in a dogmatic creed or structure—the role is filled by depth psychology. As far as analysis helps confession, it can bring about a kind of renewal. Again and again, patients dream of analysis as a refreshing and purifying bath, or other symbols of rebirth appear in their dreams and visions.[15] The knowledge of what is going on in their unconscious gives them renewed vitality.

Jung purposely did not develop a systematic therapeutic method or technique, as did Freud and others. But Jung did describe four characteristic stages of the analytic process: confession, elucidation, education and transformation.[16]

In the first stage, you get things off your chest. Its prototype is the confessional practice of almost all the mystery religions of antiquity and their historical continuation in the Catholic Church. You confess to the analyst everything consciously concealed, repressed, guilt-laden, etc.—thoughts, wishes, fantasies, emotions like fear, hate, aggression and so on, and whatever else you are not proud of.

In the second stage, *elucidation,* you become aware of personal unconscious contents that have not been concealed or repressed but rather have never been conscious—dormant character traits, attitudes and abilities. You develop an understanding of complexes, projection, persona and shadow, anima and animus, and become aware of a regulating center, which Jung called the Self. This comes about mainly through close attention to your responses to daily events and the nightly images that surface in your dreams.

Once these contents have been assimilated to consciousness, the

---

[15] See, for instance, Marie-Louise von Franz, *Redemption Motifs in Fairy Tales,* pp. 21ff.

[16] See "Problems of Modern Psychotherapy," *The Practice of Psychotherapy,* CW 16, pars. 122ff.; also Marie-Louise von Franz, *C.G. Jung: His Myth in Our Time,* pp. 66ff.

next task is that of *education,* which refers to discovering your role as a social being—your place in the world, where you fit in, your vocation. You do not exist in a vacuum; you are a significant cog in the cosmic community we call humankind.

In the fourth stage, *transformation,* you become more fully the person you were always meant to be. Unconscious compulsion is replaced by conscious development; aimless activity gives way to a directed focus on what is personally relevant and meaningful. Egocentricity is subsumed by a working relationship with the Self, or, as it has been called, one's original "greater personality." This is a term Jung introduced in his essay "Concerning Rebirth," where he speaks of individuation as "a long-drawn-out process of inner transformation and rebirth into another being." He goes on:

> This "other being" is the other person in ourselves—that larger and greater personality maturing within us . . . the inner friend of the soul. . . . into whom Nature herself would like to change us—that other person who we also are and yet can never attain to completely. . . . We should prefer to be always "I" and nothing else. But we are confronted with that inner friend or foe, and whether he is our friend or foe depends on ourselves.[17]

Friend or foe? What an interesting question, for our greater personality often thwarts our conscious will, thus appearing to be a malicious antagonist, though he or she is not that at all.

The above process of maturation—from confession to transformation—although not the only possible sequence, is essentially what Jung meant by individuation. It takes time and effort and usually involves some sacrifices along the way, but it can happen.

In addition, the encounter with the greater personality within can be, writes Jung, "a moment of deadliest peril."[18] This realization may be a shock to those who imagine that individuation is the answer to all their problems, as if becoming who one is meant to be is

---

[17] *The Archetypes and the Collective Unconscioous,* CW 9i, par. 235.

[18] Ibid., par. 217.

a goal like losing that extra twenty pounds or running a marathon.

Encountering one's greater personality is perilous because it can change everything—the way we see ourselves and others, and the way we live. The questions, "Who am I?" and "What am I doing?" commonly surface, and then life becomes more complicated, more problematic. Elsewhere Jung puts it like this: *"The experience of the self is always a defeat for the ego,"*[19]—like discovering that the earth revolves around the sun and not vice versa.—and so there is bound to be chaos, confusion and uncertainty.[20]

I recently awoke to a day ahead with no commitments. I reveled in the thought of writing with no interruptions. But I could not settle to writing or to anything else. I frittered the time away, aimlessly, producing nothing. I slept and moped and watched old movies on television. At the end of the day I felt like a no-good wastrel. After a couple of days beating up on myself I had a dream which gave me a new perspective on that experience. I saw my inability to do anything useful as the work of the self-regulating function of the psyche; which is to say I needed to slow down. The Self stepped in and reminded me that I wasn't in charge.

I could give other examples, all illustrating the fact that in the long run, the ego must take second place to the Self, whose dictates, however unwelcome to the ego, are essentially in the service of individuation. Acknowledging that the inner Self is equivalent to the Judeo-Christian God of the Old Testament, one of Jung's most radical ideas is that the Self (a.k.a. God) needs humanity to become conscious. This notion he espouses convincingly and at great length in his essay, "Answer to Job."[21]

---

[19] *Mysterium Coniunctionis,* CW 14, par. 778.

[20] For in-depth accounts of the experience, see Edward F. Edinger, *Encounter with the Self: A Jungian Commentary on* William Blake's *Illustrations of the Book of Job;* also Edinger, "Encounter with the Greater Personality," in *Science of the Soul: A Jungian Perspective,* pp. 40ff.

[21] *Psychology and Religion: West and East,* CW 11, pars. 553ff. (also published separately). See also Edward F. Edinger, *Transformation of the God-Image: An Elucidation of Jung's "Answer to Job."*

There are many methods and techniques taught by therapists of different schools, but Jung's view was that technique is not important. What matters is rather the analyst's self-knowledge and continuing attention to his or her own unconscious. Analysis is in fact both a craft and an art. Whatever school an analyst trains in, he or she is obliged to deal in an individual way with who comes in the door. Jung said that when a unique, suffering person was in front of him, he put theory on the shelf and just listened. Nor did he insist on analyzing the unconscious, believing that consistent support of the conscious attitude is often enough to bring about satisfactory results. So long as it does not obtrude itself, Jung felt, the unconscious is best left alone. Depth analysis is like a surgical operation; one should only resort to the knife when other methods have failed.

Nobody can be absolutely right in either the physical sciences or the practice of psychology. The tool with which we interpret what happens in both the material world and the psyche is the psyche itself. The observer's psychological predispositions and hypotheses influence what is observed; matter in the outer world and psyche in the inner are not only objects of investigation, but also subjects.[22] It is a circular process with few objective guidelines, and so analysts of any school must be very modest in what they claim to do.

Today there are so many psychological theories that psychotherapy is a bewildering quagmire. The Freudian and Adlerian schools are only two of the most well known of the depth psychologies. There is also the Kleinian school and the Kohutians; there are Reichians, Lacanians, Hillmanians, Primal Screamers and Mindellians. There are those who work with sand, paint, clay, smell, palms, handwriting, aromas and bumps on the head; while others still put their faith in abreaction or hypnosis. That is only in the psychodynamic area. There are also psychiatrists, behaviorists, neurologists, teachers, linguists, theologians and philosophers who blithely overstep their limits in calling themselves psychologists.

---

[22] See J. Gary Sparks, *At the Heart of Matter: Synchronicity and Jung's Spiritual Testament,* pp. 12ff.

In short, psychology is a point of view and no one theory explains everything. At the same time, it is very important that therapists believe in their particular approach, for, as Jung pointed out, it is often *that* one believes, not *what,* which has a curative effect.

That being said, Jung's understanding of the psyche seems to appeal to those who are philosophically minded and function reasonably well in outer life. They have inner conflicts and problems in relationships, which of course they rationalize as best they can, but on the whole they are no more neurotic than the rest of us. They are grateful to learn about the ubiquitous influence of the unconscious and are open to a mythological and symbolic perspective. Much of this they can find in books. The next step, personal analysis, is best suited to those who have reached the end of their tether and have no place else to go, or are otherwise called to focus on their inner journey.

Self-knowledge can be the antidote to a pervasive malaise, a world-weariness particularly common in middle age, and a spur to an adventurous inner life—the so-called hero's journey.[23] Understanding yourself is also a matter of asking the right questions, again and again. Do that for long enough and the capital-S Self, one's regulating center, is activated. That's when you realize that your ego is answerable to a higher authority, your greater personality—an inner center with virtually all the authority and failings of the Biblical God, but inside and not in the great beyond.

Marie-Louise von Franz, doyenne of Jungian analysts until her death in 1998, writes that having a relationship with the Self is like being in touch with an "instinct of truth." There is an immediate awareness of what is right and true, a truth without reflection:

> One reacts rightly without knowing why, it flows through one and one does the right thing. . . . With the help of the instinct of truth, life goes on as a meaningful flow, as a manifestation of the Self.[24]

---

[23] See commentaries in my books: *The Survival Papers,* pp. 77ff., and *Jungian Psychology Unplugged: My Life as an Elephant,,* pp. 107ff.

[24] *Alchemy: An Introduction to the Symbolism and the Psychology,* pp. 172f.

In practical terms, this comes down to simply knowing what is right for oneself. One has a strong instinctive feeling of what should be and what could be. To depart from this leads to error, aberration and illness—and to hiding under the covers.

Personally, I owe my life to depth psychology and to the application of Jung's ideas. Once upon a time I was on my knees. After a few years of analysis I could again walk. One day, perhaps, I will jog, or even run. Meanwhile, I truck along with the elephants and keep track of my feces.

4

Some Crucial Points in Psychoanalysis:
A Correspondence between Dr. Jung and Dr. Loÿ
(from *Freud and Psychoanalysis,* CW 4; vintage 1917)

(Loÿ:) You conceive the tasks of psychoanalysis to be much deeper than I had ever imagined: it is no longer a question of getting rid of troublesome pathological symptoms, but of the analysand learning to know himself completely—not just his anxiety experiences—and on the basis of this knowledge building up and shaping his life anew. But he himself must be the builder; the analyst only furnishes him with the necessary tools.[25]

(Jung:)When once psychoanalysis has been applied in a suitable case, it is *imperative* that rational solutions of the conflicts should be found. The objection is at once advanced that many conflicts are intrinsically insoluble. People sometimes take this view because they think only of external solutions—which at bottom are not solutions at all. If a man cannot get on with his wife, he naturally thinks the conflict would be solved if he married someone else. When such marriages are examined they are seen to be no solution whatever. The old Adam enters upon the new marriage and bungles it just as badly as he did the earlier one. A real solution comes only from within and then only because the patient has been brought to a different attitude.[26]

I was in tears re-reading these passages for about the twentieth time, for I have so often experienced their truth.

The implication is clear: only through self-understanding is it possible to have a harmonious relationship. But even so, there is no end of pickles people get into.

---

[25] "Some Crucial Points in Psychoanalysis: A Correspondence between Dr. Jung and Dr. Loÿ," *Freud and Psychoanalysis,* CW 4, par. 576. Dr. Loÿ was in analysis with Jung at the time.

[26] Ibid., par. 606.

A relationship, although it may be experimental, is not a scientific experiment, where you end up with a foreseen result—Q.E.D, it's called in Latin: *quod erat demonstrandum* (that which was to be proved). That was an important tenet in my early education, and for years I took that principle into life, but in the end it just didn't work, and so no more. Logos has long since given way in my life to Eros. I no longer have to prove anything. I just have to honor how I feel, which as it happens is not really easier than proving a hypothesis in physics. But I can tell you, it sure is more satisfying.

I am reminded of Jung's admonition to a client who complained that he was always on bad terms with his wife and others he loved. Here it is:

> Of course, it is most regrettable that you always get into trouble but don't you see what you are doing? You love somebody, you identify with them, and of course you prevail against the objects of your love and repress them by your very self-evident identity. You handle them as if they were yourself, and naturally there will be resistances. It is a violation of the individuality of those people, and it is a sin against your own individuality. Those resistances are a most useful and important instinct: you have resistances, scenes, and disappointments so that you may become finally conscious of yourself, and then hatred is no more.[27]

Of course Jung is touching here on the fact of projection, which regularly facilitates relationships with others at the same time as it lays the groundwork for undermining them.

Projection—now this is a very pesky topic. But I'll have a go. Briefly, I think projection is everything, the alpha and omega, of relationship. There is hardly a man or woman in the world, from the halt, the lame and the blind to the most beautiful, who cannot spark someone's love or hate through the psychological phenomenon of projection—often to the later bewilderment of one or both. This is neither good nor bad; it is simply life as we know it, and behind it

---

[27] Soni Shamdasani, ed., *The Psychology of Kundalini Yoga: Notes of the Seminar Given in 1932 by C.G. Jung*, p. 7.

stand all our complexes, the triggers that cause us to be attracted to, or repulsed by, another person.

We are naturally inclined to believe that the world is as we see it, that people are who we imagine them to be. However, we often learn that this is not so, because other people frequently turn out to be completely different from the way we thought they were. If they are not particularly close, we may think no more about it. But if this experience involves one of our intimates, we can be devastated.

Jung was among the first to point out that we are constantly projecting the contents of our unconscious into our environment; which is to say, we see unacknowledged aspects of ourselves in other people. In this way we create a series of imaginary relationships that often have little or nothing to do with the others. Indeed, given the right circumstances, there is no end to what we may project onto others—mother, father, hero, artist, guru; you name it, we can project it.

No one can escape this. It is quite normal for unconscious contents to be projected. That is an inescapable fact of life. Projection has generally had a bad press, but in its positive sense it creates an agreeable bridge between people, facilitating friendship and communication. Like the persona, projection greases the wheels of social intercourse. And as with complexes, life would be a whole lot duller without projection.

Unfortunately, projection can also create a gulf between people, which often happens, for instance, between those in different political camps or religions. It is commonplace to project stupidity, or even evil, onto those we don't agree with.

We can also project onto things. This used to be known as having a fetish and was generally considered to be unhealthy. People laughed at you if you had a fascination for, say, shoes or buttons or, well, elephants. They still do, of course, but nowadays some of us know that such things have a symbolic, psychological meaning. For behind projections are their motivating force, so to speak—our complexes, which predispose us to like or dislike others. It is a dog's breakfast, and we would be wise to become aware of it.

There is passive projection and there is active projection. Passive projection is completely automatic and unintentional. For instance, our eyes catch another's across a crowded room and we are smitten, head over heels; or the opposite, instant dislike. We may know nothing about that person; in fact the less we know, the easier it is to project. We fill the void with ourselves.

Active projection is also called empathy. You feel yourself into the other's shoes by imagining what he or she is going through. This is an essential ability for an analyst. Without it there is a long succession of boring days with uninteresting people who have unimaginable problems. With it, you're constantly on the edge.

There is a very thin line between empathy and identification. Identification presupposes no separation between subject and object, no difference between me and the other person. We are two peas in a pod. What is good for me must be good for him—or her. Many relationships run aground on this mistaken notion. It is the motivation for much well-meaning advice to others, and the premise of any therapeutic system relying on suggestion or adaptation to collectively sanctioned behavior and ideals.

Therapy conducted on this basis can do more harm than good. That is why Jung insisted that those in training to become analysts must have a thorough personal analysis before being let loose. Only through an intimate knowledge of my own complexes and predispositions can I know where I end and the other begins. And even then I can't always be sure. When someone whose psychology is similar to mine shows up, I really have to be careful.

In relationships, identification is as common as potatoes and always spells trouble. When you identify with another person, your emotional well-being is intimately linked with the mood of that person and his or her attitude toward you. The psychology of such a situation is succinctly expressed in that old popular song, "I Want To Be Happy / But I Can't Be Happy / Till I Make You Happy Too." Of course, this is a natural feeling, but the thrust of the individuation process is often *contra naturam* (against nature), which means that many "natural" feelings may have to be overcome.

Now, I am as prone as anyone else to be caught in such a mutually destructive mind-set, but at least I try to keep my wits about me, constantly reminding myself that my loved others are genuinely "other" and that their problems are not mine.

Emotional interdependence is a classic double-bind. You can't function independently and your dependence has the effect of making the other person responsible for how *you* feel. More: you have a relationship that is psychologically the same as that between parent and child. Worse: at any given moment it is hard to tell which partner is parent and which is child. Such a situation is psychologically untenable in the long run. Neither can make a move without double-thinking the effect on the other, which automatically inhibits the self-expression of both.

Projection, if it doesn't slide into identification, is actually quite useful. When we assume that some quality or characteristic is present in another, and then, through experience, find that this is not true, we are obliged to realize that the world is not our personal creation. If we are reflective, we can learn something about ourselves. This process is called withdrawing projections. It doesn't happen overnight, and it's usually quite painful.

It only becomes necessary to withdraw projections when our expectations of others are frustrated. If there is no obvious disparity between what we expect, or imagine to be true, and the reality we are faced with, there is no need to withdraw projections. Don't look a gift horse in the mouth; let sleeping dogs lie—as long as they do.

Also on the positive side, it must be said that projection can constellate unrealized or dormant qualities in another person. Parental expectations notoriously lead one astray, but they can also be the stimulus to explore one's potential. Also, many a grown woman has achieved more than she might have without a friend's injunction: "You can do it!" And many a man owes his accomplishments to similar urgings from a loving mate. As long as power over the other, or one's own unlived life, is not lurking in the shadows, such projections do no harm at all.

In this correspondence Jung also disdains the efficacy of suggestion as a therapeutic tool:

> I can say that I adopt the following standpoint: every procedure is good if it helps. I therefore acknowledge every method of suggestion including Christian Science, mental healing, etc. "A truth is a truth, when it works." It is another question, though, whether a scientifically trained doctor can square it with his conscience to sell little bottles of Lourdes water because this suggestion is at times very helpful. Even the so-called highly scientific suggestion therapy employs the wares of the medicine man and the exorcising shaman. And why not? The public is not much more advanced either and continues to expect miraculous cures from the doctor. And indeed, we must rate those doctors wise—worldly–wise in every sense— who know how to surround themselves with the aura of a medicineman.[28]

In several letters, Jung explains in detail why he abandoned hypnosis therapy as unscientific and lost faith in catharthis. He proclaims the need for anyone doing psychotherapy to undergo a personal analysis (a requirement that survives today in all Jungian training centers):

> Because I know that, despite all rational safeguards, the patient does attempt to assimilate the analyst's personality, I have laid it down as a requirement that the psychotherapist must be just as responsible for the cleanness of his hands as the surgeon. I even hold it to be an indispensable prerequisite that the psychoanalyst should first submit himself to the analytical process, as his personality is one of the main factors in the cure.
>
> Patients read the analyst's character intuitively, and they should find in him a man with failings, admittedly, but also a man who strives at every point to fulfil his human duties in the fullest sense.

---

[28] "Some Crucial Points in Psychoanalysis: *Freud and Psychoanalysis,* CW 4, par. 578.

Many times I have had the opportunity of seeing that the analyst is successful with his treatment just so far as he has succeeded in his own moral development.[29]

Personal moral development! Now here was something not previously asked of doctors or indeed expected of anyone dealing with the psyches of others. The Biblical injunction, "Physician, heal thyself" (Luke 4:23) was not a popular moral admonition until the advent of modern depth psychology.

Regarding morality and Jung's views about conflict cited at the beginning of this chapter, the following passage is particularly relevant:

If an external solution is possible no psychoanalysis is necessary; but if an internal solution is sought, we are faced with the peculiar task of psychoanalysis. The conflict between "love and duty" must be solved on that level of character where "love and duty" are no longer opposites, which in reality they are not. Similarly, the familiar conflict between "instinct and conventional morality" must be solved in such a way that both factors are taken sufficiently into account, and this again is possible only through a change of character. This change psychoanalysis can bring about. In such cases external solutions are worse than none at all.[30]

In one letter, Jung presents this clear and succinct description of what psychoanalysis is and can do:

Psychoanalysis is first of all simply a method—but a method complying with all the rigorous requirements which the concept of a "method" implies today. Let me say at once that psychoanalysis is not an *anamnesis* [case history], as those who know everything without learning it are pleased to believe. It is essentially a way of investigating unconscious associations which cannot be got at by exploring the conscious mind. Again, psychoanalysis is not a

---

[29] Ibid., pars. 586f.

[30] Ibid., par. 607. This passage seems to foreshadow Jung's concept of the transcendent function, the "third not given" that unites the opposites, as elucidated below in chap. 8.

method of examination in the nature of an intelligence test, though this mistake is common in certain circles. Nor is it a method of catharsis for abreacting, with or without hypnosis, real or imaginary traumata.

Psychoanalysis is a method which makes possible the analytical reduction of psychic contents to their simplest expression, and for discovering the line of least resistance in the development of a harmonious personality. . . .

The main principle of psychoanalytic technique is to analyse the psychic contents that present themselves at a given moment. So-called chance is the law and order of psychoanalysis.[31]

Jung goes on to emphasize that every analysis develops differently and individually, so it is not possible to give rules or recipes of procedure. He elaborates in a later letter:

The line of least resistance does not signify *eo ipso* the avoidance of pain so much as the just balancing of pain and pleasure. Painful activity by itself leads to no result but exhaustion. A man must be able to enjoy life, otherwise the effort of living is not worth while.

What direction the patient's life should take in the future is not ours to judge. We must not imagine that we know better than his own nature, or we would prove ourselves educators of the worst kind. . . . Psychoanalysis is only a means for removing the stones from the path of development, and not a method (as hypnotism often claims to be) of putting things into the patient that were not there before. It is better to renounce any attempt to give direction, and simply try to throw into relief everything that the analysis brings to light, so that the patient can see it clearly and be able to draw suitable conclusions. Anything he has not acquired himself he will not believe in the long run, and what he takes over from authority merely keeps him infantile. He should rather be put in a position to take his own life in hand. The art of analysis lies in following the patient on all his erring ways and so gathering his strayed sheep together.[32]

---

[31] Ibid., pars. 622ff.
[32] Ibid., pars. 642f.

I love that reference to "strayed sheep" as a metaphor for complexes that mill about in a vast field awaiting their Miss Bo-Peep—the ego—to direct their aimless energy to meaningful ends.

And that, in a few words, is the aim of Jungian analysis—to bring to light and help facilitate the natural flow of the patient's energy. No one can direct so-called disposable energy at will. It follows its own gradient. As Jung expresses it elsewhere:

> Life can flow forward only along the path of the gradient. But there is no energy unless there is a tension of opposites; hence it is necessary to discover the opposite to the attitude of the conscious mind. . . The conscious mind is on top, the shadow underneath, and just as high always longs for low and hot for cold, so all consciousness, perhaps without being aware of it, seeks its unconscious opposite, lacking which it is doomed to stagnation, congestion, and ossification. Life is born only of the spark of opposites.[33]

Personally, I don't count sheep to fall asleep; I count the pickles my shadow has got me into—and sometimes out of.

---

[33] "The Problem of the Attitude-type," *Two Essays on Anaytical Psychology,* CW 7, par. 78.

5
Two Kinds of Thinking
(from *Symbols of Transformation,* CW 5;
vintage 1912/1950)

Almost every day we can see for ourselves, when falling asleep, how our fantasies get woven into our dreams, so that between day-dreaming and night-dreaming there is not much difference. We have therefore two kinds of thinking: directed thinking, and dreaming or fantasy-thinking. The former operates with speech elements for the purpose of communication, and is difficult and exhausting; the latter is effortless, working as it were spontaneously, with the contents ready to hand, and guided by unconscious motives.

. . . . The clearest expression of modern directed thinking is science and the techniques fostered by it. Both owe their existence simply and solely to energetic training in directed thinking.[34]

Any lessening of interest, or the slightest fatigue, is enough to put an end to the delicate psychological adaptation to reality which is expressed through directed thinking, and to replace it by fantasies.[35]

What, with us, crops up only in dreams and fantasies was once either a conscious custom or a general belief. But what was once strong enough to mould the spiritual life of a highly developed people will not have vanished without trace from the human soul in the course of a few generations. We must remember that a mere eighty generations separate us from the Golden Age of Greek culture.[36]

Whereas directed thinking is an altogether conscious phenom-

---

[34] "Two Kinds of Thinking," *Symbols of Transformation,* CW 5, pars. 20f.
[35] Ibid., par. 32.
[36] Ibid., par. 35.

enon, the same cannot be said of fantasy-thinking. Much of it belongs to the conscious sphere, but at least as much goes on in the
half-shadow, or entirely in the unconscious, and can therefore be
inferred only indirectly. Through fantasy-thinking, directed thinking is brought into contact with the oldest layers of the human
mind, long buried beneath the threshold of consciousness. The
fantasy-products directly engaging the conscious mind are, first
of all, waking dreams or daydreams . . . . then ordinary dreams,
which present to the conscious mind a baffling exterior and only
make sense on the basis of indirectly inferred unconscious contents. Finally, in split-off complexes there are completely unconscious fantasy-systems that have a marked tendency to constitute
themselves as separate personalities.[37]

Symbols of Transformation signaled Jung's definitive break with
Freud, for in it Jung explicitly distanced himself from Freud's
dogmatic view that all neuroses derived from sexual problems in
childhood, naming the Oedipus and Electra complexes as the major
culprits that informed and interfered with later relationships.

Freud wrote of "libido" exclusively in terms of sexuality. Jung
redefined libido as multifaceted psychic energy, which could manifest in myriad symbolic ways, as evidenced in the fantasies of the
pseudonymous Miss Frank Miller—the subject matter of this *CW*
volume—which prompted Jung to explore the significance of age-
old mythological and religious themes that were still alive in the
psyches of modern men and women.[38] This was the genesis of
Jung's concept of the collective unconscious, an inherited stratum
of the psyche that manifests collectively in myth and religion, and
subjectively in the dreams and fantasies of individuals.

---

[37] Ibid., par. 39.

[38] Jung did not know or ever meet Miss Miller. He became aware of her fantasies
through their publication in 1906 by the then-eminent Theodore Flournoy under
the title "Quelques faits d'imagination créatice subconsciente." An English translation of the fantasies, without commentary, is given as an appendix in CW 5 under
the title, "Some Instances of Subconscious Creative Imagination."

In Jung's preamble to his discussion of Miss Miller's fantasies, he distinguishes between directed thinking and fantasy or dream thinking, as noted in the passages above. In aid of his views, he elicits the support of scholars, linguists, philosophers and mythologists. There is a consensus, he shows, that there are indeed "two kinds of thinking."

In short, dream/fantasy thinking is what assails us at night or surprises us at odd times of day. Directed thinking is akin to what we nowadays call linear thinking. It is entirely straightforward, logical and rational; it moves from A to B to C and so on, whereas fantasy thinking hops about intuitively, apparently at random (like lateral thinking). Directed thinking sticks to the highway; fantasy thinking favors the byway.

But that is just the beginning. The rest of this volume, *Symbols of Transformation,* is an astonishingly imaginative, intuitive trek through the worlds of mythology, religion and individual psychology—indeed, a prime example of a melding of the two kinds of thinking, for Jung's intuitive amplifications of dream images always come back down to earth with pointed, directed thinking showing their significance in the context of a person's everyday life. It makes for exciting reading—at once heady and earthy.

Let us not confuse dream/fantasy thinking with so-called magical thinking, which flourished in the Middle Ages. The former is rooted in reality; magical thinking involves the primitive belief that your thoughts can change what happens in the world around you—the basis for all kinds of witchery: curses, blessings and love charms. .

What Jung does in this essay truly boggles the time- and space-bound mind. Here is an example:.

> But just where do the fantasies get their material? Let us take as an example a typical adolescent fantasy. Faced by the vast uncertainty of the future, the adolescent puts the blame for it on the past, saying to himself, "If only I were not the child of my very ordinary parents, but the child of a rich and elegant count and had merely been brought up by foster-parents, then one day a golden coach would come and the count would take his long-lost child back with him to

his wonderful castle, and so on, just as in a Grimms' fairy-story which a mother tells her children. With a normal child the fantasy stops short of the fleeting idea, which is soon over and forgotten. There was a time, however, in the ancient world, when the fantasy was a legitimate truth that enjoyed universal recognition. The heroes—Romulus and Remus, Moses, Semiramis, and many others—were foundlings whose real parents had lost them. Others were directly descended from the gods, and the noble families traced their descent from the heroes and gods of old. Hence the fantasy of our adolescent is simply a re-echo of an ancient folk-belief which was once very widespread. The fantasy of ambition therefore chooses, among other things, a classical form which at one time had real value. The same is true of certain erotic fantasies.[39]

Now, wouldn't that encourage you to look at your teenage son or daughter in a different light? I mean, they are under the influence of primordial forces, so give them some slack.

The movement from directed to fantasy thinking often occurs when the level of consciousness is lowered, as commonly happens when we are fatigued, ill, under the influence of alcohol or other drugs, or erotically engaged.

It is arguably fortunate that directed thinking often gives way to fantasy thinking involving love and sex, or how else could the world go round? I have been with women who liked being loved but could not return it. I have been with women who loved and I could not. There have been casual encounters and some more serious, but in retrospect I see them all in terms of educating my anima as to who would be a suitable mate.[40] For you see, without my inner woman's cooperation I am a tin man without a heart. There, I just slipped into fantasy thinking.

I was brought up in the United Church of Canada, which is pretty sparse on ritual, but I did learn some hymns that still have the

---

[39] Ibid., par. 34.

[40] This may only make sense if you believe in Darwin's theory of evolution, as I do.

power to move me, like Sarah Vaughn's rendition of *The Lord's Prayer*. I don't know if it's the words or the music, but I cry. It's another just-so story and I don't question it.

Moving on with erotic fantasies, I have a reasonably good idea of what constellates a man's desire for a woman, but I am pretty fuzzy on what sparks a woman's desire for a particular man. Money, power, status, appearance? All that is just on the surface. What arouses the feeling that, according to a classic song, "I'm in the mood for love / simply because you're near me"? What makes her tingle?

√ I used to be puzzled too by the fact that a woman could say she loved a man but didn't desire him. Few men are mature enough to make that distinction, but it seems to be natural for women. I have known some women in that situation, which became problematic only when they came across a man they did desire, naturally creating a conflict—which in the Jungian view is all to the good, for wrestling with opposing forces in the psyche promotes a more comprehensive consciousness of ourselves. Recall the Biblical Jacob, who wrestled with an angel until dawn. The angel finally conceded defeat and blessed Jacob by renaming him "Israel." Did that really happen, or is it a fantastic fable? Never mind, it is a cornerstone in the history of the Jews, and that is real enough.

Classical psychoanalytic—and Jungian—theory holds that a woman's choice of a mate has a lot to do with her early-life relationship with her father. She may favor someone like him, or just the opposite. Jungian theory also suggests that a psychologically naive woman will be attracted to a man of physical prowess; that a more psychologically mature woman will favor a man of some mental stature with creative ideas; and that a man of apparent wisdom will win the heart of a woman who has experientially differentiated her personal psychology. I don't know, but Marie-Louise von Franz puts it like this:

> The animus, just like the anima, exhibits four stages of development.
> He first appears as a personification of mere physical power—for

instance, as an athletic champion or "muscle man." In the next stage he possesses initiative and the capacity for planned action. In the third phase the animus becomes the "word," often appearing as a professor or clergyman. Finally, in his fourth manifestation, the animus is the incarnation of *meaning*. On this highest level he becomes (like the anima) a mediator of the religious experience whereby life acquires new meaning.[41]

It is posited too that a favored outer man is often a reflection of, or embodies, a woman's inner masculine, her animus in projection, as it were, just as an outer woman may personify a man's anima.

I asked my loverNot, Nurse Pam, about this. She blinked her big green eyes and said, "I respond to a man who knows himself and can appreciate who I am."

Great. My paramour (MP) was more circumspect: "I don't have a lot of experience in such matters. I want you just because you're you."

Projection? Probably, but I welcome it as her truth.

Me: "Are you giving yourself to me, or am I taking you?"

She: "Silly Billy, they go together, like wind and weather."

I don't know, maybe it's not so complicated for a man, and just as clear-cut as Leonard Cohen's "Suzanne":

Suzanne takes you down to a place by the river.
You can hear the boats go by,
and you can spend the night forever.
You know that she's half crazy
and that's why you want to be there.
And she feeds you tea and oranges
that come all the way from China.
And just when you mean to tell her that you have no love
to give her,
She gets you on her wavelength,

---

[41] "The Process of Individuation," in Jung and von Franz, eds., *Man and His Symbols,* p. 194. The four analogous stages in a man's erotic development are Eve (mother), Helen (lover), Mary (soulful friend) and Sophia (wisdom).

And she lets the river answer
that you've always been her lover.
And you want to travel with her,
And you want to travel blind,
And you know that she will trust you,
For you touched her perfect body with your mind.
   And she shows you where to look
between the garbage and the flowers.
There are heroes in the seaweed
there are children in the moment
They are leaning out for love,
and they will lean that way forever,
While Suzanne holds the mirror.

   . . . . .

She's wearin' rags and feathers from
Salvation Army counters
And the sun showers down. like honey
on our lady of the harbor.
and she shows you where to look
between the garbage and the flowers.
There are heroes in the seaweed,
there are children in the moment
They are leaning out for love,
and they will lean that way forever,
   But Suzanne holds the mirror.
   And you want to travel with her
   And you want to travel blind
   because you think that you can trust her,
   for you've touched her perfect body with your mind
   While Suzanne holds the mirror.[42]

Cohen's poem/song may have originated in a real-life encounter, but for most men "Suzanne" is a fantasy lover who never was or might yet be. A man's unconscious is a harem, teeming with so many enticing images of the feminine that he often forgets his lady

---

[42] Nina Simone version. © BMG Music

love right in front of his face. And so, come to that, might she. There are many reasons why couples split up, but a common deal-breaker is that one partner takes the other for granted and loses sight of how and why they came together in the first place. Natalie Cole sings it like this:

> *Non dimenticar*
> means don't forget you are
> My dar-ling.
> Don't forget to be
> All you mean to me
> *Non dimenticar.*
>
> My love is like a star
> My dar-ling
> Shining bright and clear
> Just because you're near.
>
> Please do not forget
> That our lips have met
> And I've held you tightly.
> Was it dreams ago
> My heart felt it glow
> Or only just tonight dear?
> *Non dimenticar*
>
> Although you've traveled far
> My dar-ling
> It's my heart you own
> So I will wait alone
> *Non dimenticar.*[43]

Even a happily married man may be tempted to romp with another woman, which is to say his instinctive shadow taps his shoulder and wants to come out to play. I imagine this happens with women too, for desire is a manifestation of psychic energy and not a monopoly of either gender. So, in commenting on such matters

---

[43] *"Noon dimenticar."* Lyrics by Shelley Dobbins. © BMI.

one better not generalize, for notwithstanding any theory, the attraction between a man and a woman is usually more individual than collective.

·Perhaps the major problem between men and women today is that a woman wants to be seen in her entirety, and men persist in seeing her simply as an object of lust—or the flip side, as mother. Many women apparently enjoy being lusted after, even invite it by dressing or acting provocatively. We can probably thank the multi-billion-dollar fashion industry for that. But women of some maturity, though they may appreciate being desired, rightly resent being objectified. As for the flip side, it is virtually a given that over time a man will turn his lover into his mother—and she may enjoy that too, given the power that goes with it. It is a sad fact that courtship often ends when a woman surrenders her heart and her body. Men are easily bored by women's prattle, their fears and vanities, even their ambitions, and generally lack the patience to relate to their partners as independent human beings. Magazines are full of good advice on keeping romance alive, but desire is a murkier matter.

The foregoing may be objectively true or just my personal experience, but anyway, I do know that I am as prone as any man to treat a woman as an object. This is overtly encouraged by Western culture, where sex is the ubiquitous coin of the realm, and attractive, nubile women are the standard-bearers. I can be seduced by such images. However, I try to counter my chauvinist tendencies by encouraging my sweetheart to tell me of her daily activities and feelings, her opinions, triumphs and woes. I revel in the minutiae of her life. In this way I get to know her as a substantial other and not just a projected fantasy. And she, in fact, returns the favor, as it were. This works, more or less. The courtship goes on and on, and mutually loving feelings are enhanced.[44] Physical beauty attracts my attention, but my heart is a harder nut to crack.

---

[44] My Romance Trilogy *(Not the Big Sleep, On Staying Awake* and *Eyes Wide Open)* covers most of the bases on this subject. Here I am just tying up a few loose ends.

"Suzanne holds the mirror"—indeed, I think that for most men she *is* the mirror, which is to say, a reflection of themselves. That may or may not be so, but as much as it is true, it is a good day-to-day example of dream/fantasy-thinking. We see ourselves in others, and that is alternately enlivening and depressing. But it is also life.

And of course it's not all bad. Through fantasy-thinking we get to know ourselves in a way that is inhibited by directed thinking. Flights of fancy are ubiquitous in the still of the night, and we are well advised to take note of them in the light of day, lest they overtake us from behind.

Alright, so some of the foregoing is rather facetious on my part. I mean, the complex diversity of relationships between men and women will probably always remain a mystery, theory be damned. But if enough men and women speak their truth instead of fudging it to save face or keep the peace, we may yet get closer to the heart of the matter. We may theorize and academically obfuscate until the cows come home, but in the long run personal experience will carry the day.

"A truth is a truth when it works," says Jung. Of course that isn't necessarily so because Jung said it, but it might be, and I can live with that because my own hard-won truths work; well, most of the time. And when they don't, I revise them.

Now listen to Nina Simone:

Cherish is the word I use to describe
all the feeling that I have hiding here for you inside.
You don't know how many times I've wished
that I had told you.
You don't know how many times I've wished
that I could hold you.
You don't know how many times I've wished
that I could
mold you into someone who could
cherish me as much as I cherish you.

Perish is the word that more than applies
to the hope in my heart

each time I realize
that I am not gonna be the one to share your dreams,
that I am not gonna be the one to share your schemes,
that I am not gonna be the one to share what
seems to be the life that you could
cherish as much as I do yours.

Oh I'm beginning to think that man has
never found
the words that could
make you want me,
that have the right amount of letters, just
the right sound,
that could make you
hear, make you see
That you are drivin' me out of my mind.

Cherish is the word I
use to describe
all the feeling that I
have hiding here for you inside.
You don't know how many times I've wished
that I had told you.
You don't know how many times I've wished
that I could hold you.
You don't know how many times I've wished
that I could
mold you into someone who could
cherish me as much as
I cherish you.
And I do cherish you
Cherish is the word[45]

Well, that's very romantic, as am I. The very idea of romance animates me, keeps me up at night. That is fantasy thinking, for sure, but writing about it requires directed thinking.

Being in love is very exciting. I've been there, lived that, perhaps

---

[45] "Cherish," Lyrics by Oscar Hammerstein II, B. Kalmar, H. Ruby. © EMI Miller.

a dozen times—the magic, the yearning, the aching desire, the lonely, jealous nights, the painful ecstasy—and then the painful let-down, the brush-off, the self-pity, lonelier nights and self-doubts. But I wouldn't forsake the magic for all the oil in Texas. It's quite simple—life is rosier, more fun, when you're in love, no matter that the end is foreseeable. And after the fading of desire, there is al-ways the possibility of a sustainable, loving relationship with a companionable other who accepts the dolt that you are.

Okay, while we're here, we might as well add Rod Stewart to the mix, and why not? Jung's wine cellar was our starting point, but perhaps that was simply a pretext for a lot of other stuff to help us feel alive. Here's Rod doing an old standard:

> Give me a kiss to build a dream on
> and my imagination will thrive upon that kiss.
> Sweetheart, I ask no more than this,
> a kiss to build a dream on
> Give me a kiss before you leave me
> and my imagination will feed my hungry heart
> Leave me one thing before we part
> A kiss to build a dream on.
> When I'm alone with my fancies, I'll be with you,
> weaving romances, and making believe they're true
> Give me your lips for just a moment
> and my imagination will make that moment live.
> Give me what you alone can give
> A kiss to build a dream on.[46]

Now I ask you, what could be more fantastic than "a kiss to build a dream on"? One could say it's based on projection, of course, but so what?—no less enlivening for that. Put it right beside romance, itself a symbolic manifestation of the archetype of life. Don't suck it up. Live it out before the light goes out.

The final chapter in *Jung Uncorked* (Book Two) deals more em-phatically with symbolic thinking. But it is worth pointing out here

---

[46] "A Kiss to Build a Dream on," Lyrics by Louis Armstrong. © Proper Records.

that symbolic thinking is analogous to fantasy thinking in that both thrive on imagination, which seems to work like magic (but not magical thinking). So here is Young Sassy (twenty-year-old Sarah Vaughan) with "It's Magic," a haunting ballad first made famous by Doris Day way back in 1948. You'd have to have a heart of stone, or be terminally cynical, not to shed a tear or two:

> You sigh, the song begins,
> You speak and I hear violins,
> It's magic.
> The stars desert the skies
> and rush to nestle in your eyes,
> It's magic.
> Without a golden wand or mystic charm,
> fantastic things happen
> when I am in your arms.
> When we walk hand in hand
> the world becomes a wonderland,
> It's magic.
> How else can I explain
> Those rainbows when there is no rain?
> It's magic.
> Why do I tell myself these things that happen
> Are all really true,
> when in my heart
> I know the magic
> Is my love for you.[47]

Ah, the wonderfully romantic songsters of the 1930s and 40s, who compensated the shadow side of that era—notably Prohibition, the Great Depression, World War Two and the Holocaust. Alas, there is no escaping the opposites, and if you go with one pole you will be blind-sided by the other. That is why Jung counseled holding the tension in a conflict situation, for if you can stand it long enough, then a "third" manifests, the so-called transcendent func-

---

[47] Lyrics by Sammy Cahn. © Proper Records.

tion, as a new attitude that resolves the situation and shows the way ahead. The storm subsides and you are at peace.[48]

Will romance, like Hush-Puppies, corsets and Humphrey Bogart, ever return? Or did it ever go away? Will the world always welcome lovers as time goes by? Here's Mister Stewart again:

> You go to my head with a smile that makes my temperature rise
> Like a summer with a thousand Julys
> You intoxicate my soul with your eyes
> Though I'm certain that this heart of mine
> Hasn't a ghost of a chance in this crazy romance
> You go to my head.[49]

So there you have it. When you focus on a task at hand, you use directed thinking. But when you tell your sweetheart that she intoxicates your soul with her eyes, or that when she speaks you hear violins, why then you have entered the magical realm of symbolic/fantasy-thinking.

Directed thinking earns us a living. Symbolic thinking feeds the soul. It is sometimes problematic, of course, knowing which is more appropriate in a given situation. The ideal is to make room in your life for both. Well, good luck and God bless. As my Mac computer says when its synapses go awry, "It's not my fault. . . "

"Do you ever wonder," I recently asked MP, "why we mean so much to each other?"

"All the time," she said. She went to the little stereo in my bedroom and chose a track on the Streisand *Greatest Hits* CD:

> Life is a moment in space
> When the dream is gone
> It's a lonelier place
> I kiss the morning goodbye
> But down inside you know
> We never know why.

---

[48] See below, chap. 8.

[49] Lyrics by J. Fred Coots and Haven Gillespie. © Haven Gillespie Music.

The road is narrow and long
When eyes meet eyes
And the feeling is strong
I turn away from the wall
I stumble and fall
But I give you it all.

I am a woman in love
And I'd do anything
To get you into my world
And hold you within
It's a right I defend
Over and over again[50]

"It's so real with you," MP whispered, slipping back into bed. "And above all, I trust you,"

Amen to that. And gulp, for I don't know how trustworthy I am Not that I personally am fickle, but my shadow is an incorrigible flirt; and I, an incurable romantic, sometimes go along with him, just to keep the peace, so to speak. Hand in glove we are; but come to think of it, who's the hand and who's the glove?

Anyway, I don't feel that admiring other women is betraying my sweetheart, but in case you think that such a thing and attendant fantasies abrogate an implicit trust between partners, let me remind you that trust and betrayal are inseparable opposites. There may be a surprise in store for you if you forget that. Here is what could be the definitive commentary on the subject, in an essay by Jungian analyst James Hillman:

> We can be truly betrayed only where we truly trust—by brothers, lovers, wives, husbands, not by enemies, not by strangers. The greater the love and loyalty, the involvement and commitment, the greater the betrayal. Trust has in it the seed of betrayal; the serpent was in the garden from the beginning, just as Eve was pre-formed in the structure around Adam's heart. Trust and the possibility of betrayal come into the world at the same moment. Wherever there is

---

[50] "Woman in Love," music and lyrics by B. Gibb, R. Gibb. © Entertainment Co.

trust in a union, the risk of betrayal becomes a real possibility. And betrayal, as a continual possibility to be lived with, belongs to trust just as doubt belongs to a living faith.[51]

Of course, that doesn't explain the "why" of betrayal, or begin to gauge the hurt of it, but it is an unusual perspective and an excellent example of directed thinking, which James Hillman, whose Eros sometimes hides under a bushel, is so good at.[52]

I will now stare at the wall and let myself sink into romantic whimsy, which helps me to center myself when I'm not sure what to say or do next. Life is a washing machine. From time to time, you need to dry out.

The other day I had a tooth extracted. My dentist told me that blood would clot at the root and soon turn into bone.

"Holy petunia!" I cried.

Blood into bone! Now, *that's* real magic.

---

[51] "Betrayal," in *Loose Ends*, p. 66.

[52] The relationship between Eros and directed thinking (or Logos) is addressed here in a later chapter.

6
The Type Problem
(from *Psychological Types,* CW 6; vintage 1925)

This book is the fruit of nearly twenty years' work in the domain of practical psychology. It grew gradually in my thoughts, taking shape from the countless impressions and experiences of a psychiatrist in the treatment of nervous illnesses, from intercourse with men and women of all social levels, from my personal dealings with friend and foe alike, and, finally, from a critique of my own psychological peculiarity.[53]

Classification does not explain the individual psyche. Nevertheless, an understanding of psychological types opens the way to a better understanding of human psychology in general.[54]

The four functions are somewhat like the four points of the compass; they are just as arbitrary and just as indispensable. . . . But one thing I must confess: I would not for anything dispense with this compass on my psychological voyages of discovery.[55]

Why do we move through life the way we do? Why are we better at some activities than others? Why do some of us prefer to be alone rather than with other people—or at a party instead of reading a book? Why don't we all function in the same way?

Jung did not develop his model of psychological types in order to label people. Rather than classify people as this or that type, he sought simply to explain the differences between the ways we function and interact with our surroundings in order to promote a better understanding of human psychology in general, and one's own way of seeing the world in particular.

After many years of research, documented at length in *Psycho-*

---

[53] "Foreword to the First Swiss Edition," *Psychological Types,* CW 6, p. xi.
[54] "Psychological Types," ibid., par. 895.
[55] "A Psychological Theory of Types," Ibid., pars. 958f.

logical Types, Jung identified eight typological groups: two personality attitudes—*introversion* and *extraversion*—and four functions—*thinking, sensation, intuition* and *feeling,* each of which may operate in an introverted or extraverted way.

In Jung's model, introversion and extraversion are psychological modes of adaptation. In the former, the movement of energy is toward the inner world. In the latter, interest is directed toward the outer world. In one case the subject (inner reality) and in the other the object (outer reality) is of primary importance. Whether one is predominately introverted or extraverted—as opposed to what one is doing at any particular time—depends on the direction one's energy naturally, and usually, flows.[56]

Each of the four functions has its special area of expertise. *Thinking* refers to the process of cognitive thought; *sensation* is perception by means of the physical sense organs; *feeling* is the function of subjective judgment or valuation; and *intuition* refers to perception via the unconscious.

Briefly, the sensation function establishes that something exists, thinking tells us what it means, feeling tells us what it's worth to us, and through intuition we have a sense of what can be done with it (the possibilities). Jung insists that no one function by itself, and neither attitude alone, is sufficient for ordering our experience of ourselves or the world around us:

> For complete orientation all four functions should contribute equally: thinking should facilitate cognition and judgment, feeling should tell us how and to what extent a thing is important or unimportant for us, sensation should convey concrete reality to us through seeing, hearing, tasting, etc., and intuition should enable us to divine the hidden possibilities in the background, since these too belong to the complete picture of a given situation.[57]

---

[56] Note that introversion is quite different from introspection, which refers to self-examination. Although introverts may have more time or inclination for introspection than do extraverts, introverts have no monopoly on psychological awareness.

[57] Ibid., par. 900. Jung acknowledged that the four orienting functions do not con-

In everyday usage, the feeling function is often confused with an emotional reaction. Emotion, academically called affect, is invariably the result of an activated complex, usually accompanied by noticeable physical symptoms. When not contaminated by a complex, feeling, in its assessment of what something is worth to us, can in fact be quite cold.

Jung's basic model, including the relationship between the four functions, is a quaternity. In the following diagram, thinking is arbitrarily placed at the top; any of the other functions might be put there, according to which one a person most favors.

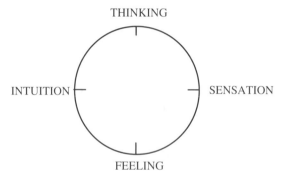

Typologically, opposites can attract or repel. Hence it is common for someone with a dominant thinking function, for instance, to be attracted to a feeling type—or shun such a person because of his or her very differentness. Similarly, intuitives may be drawn to, or distance themselves from, those with a good sensation function, and vice versa. A better understanding of these opposites—latent or dormant in ourselves—can mitigate such reactions, which often have little or nothing to do with the reality of the other person.

To my mind, Jung's model is most helpful when it is used not as a way to classify oneself or others, but rather in the way he origi-

---

tain everything in the conscious psyche. Will power and memory, for instance, are not included in his model, because although they may be affected by the way one functions typologically, they are not in themselves typological determinants.

nally thought of it, as a psychological compass. So, in any problematic situation, I ask myself four questions:

1) What are the facts? (sensation)
2) How are they linked to each other? (thinking)
3) What is it worth to me to pursue this? (feeling)
4) What are the possibilities? (intuition)

The answers aren't always clear, but the questions keep me on my toes. That is by and large why I don't favor type tests. They concretize what is inherently variable, and thereby overlook the dynamic nature of the psyche.

Any system of typology is no more than a gross indicator of what people have in common and the differences between them. Jung's model is no exception. It is distinguished solely by its parameters—the two attitudes and the four functions. What it does not and cannot show, nor does it pretend to, is the uniqueness of the individual. Also, no one is a pure type. It would be foolish to even try to reduce an individual personality to this or that, just one thing or another. Each of us is a conglomeration, an admixture of attitudes and functions that in their combination defy classification. All that is true, and emphatically acknowledged by Jung—

> One can never give a description of a type, no matter how complete, that would apply to more than one individual, despite the fact that in some ways it aptly characterizes thousands of others. Conformity is one side of a man, uniqueness is the other.[58]

—but it does not obviate the practical value of his model, particularly when one has run aground on the shoals of his or her own psychology.

Whether Jung's model is "true" or not—objectively true—is a moot point. Indeed, is anything ever "objectively" true? The real truth is that Jung's model of psychological types has all the advantages and disadvantages of any scientific model. Although lacking statistical verification, it is equally hard to disprove. But it accords

---

[58] *Psychological Types,* CW 6, par. 895.

with experiential reality. Moreover, since it is based on a fourfold—mandala-like—way of looking at things that is archetypal, it is psychologically satisfying.

As mentioned earlier, one's behavior can be quite misleading in determining typology. For instance, to enjoy being with other people is characteristic of the extraverted attitude, but this does not automatically mean that a person who enjoys lots of company is an extraverted type. Naturally, one's activities will to some extent be determined by typology, but the interpretation of those activities in terms of typology depends on the value system behind the action. Where the subject—oneself—and a personal value system are the dominant motivating factors, there is by definition an introverted type, whether at a party or alone. Similarly, when one is predominantly oriented to the object—things and other people—there is an extraverted type, whether in a crowd or on one's own. This is what makes Jung's system primarily a model of *personality* rather than of behavior.

Everything psychic is relative. I cannot say, think or do anything that is not colored by my particular way of seeing the world, which in turn is a manifestation of both my typology and my complexes. This psychological rule is analogous to Einstein's famous theory of relativity in physics, and equally as significant. Being aware of the way I tend to function makes it possible for me to assess my attitudes and behavior in a given situation and adjust them accordingly. It enables me both to compensate for my personal disposition and to be tolerant of someone who does not function as I do—someone who has, perhaps, a strength or facility I myself lack.

Typologically speaking, the important question is not whether one is innately introverted or extraverted, or which function is superior or inferior, but, more pragmatically: in *this* situation, with *that* person, how did I function and with what effect? Did my actions truly reflect my judgments (thinking and feeling) and perceptions (sensation and intuition)? And if not, why not? What complexes were activated in me? To what end? How and why did I mess things up? What does this say about my psychology? What can I do about it? What do I *want* to do about it?

These are among the questions we must take to heart if we want to be psychologically conscious.

*

According to Jung, his initial motivation for investigating typology was his need to understand why Freud's view was so different from that of Alfred Adler.

Freud saw his patients as being preeminently dependent upon, and defining themselves in relation to, significant objects, particularly the parents. Adler's emphasis was on how a person, or subject, seeks his own security and supremacy. The one supposes that human behavior is conditioned by the object, the other finds the determining agency in the subject. Jung expressed appreciation for both points of view:

> The Freudian theory is attractively simple, so much so that it almost pains one if anybody drives in the wedge of a contrary assertion. But the same is true of Adler's theory. It too is of illuminating simplicity and explains as much as the Freudian theory. . . .
>
> . . . But how comes it that each investigator sees only one side, and why does each maintain that he has the only valid view? . . . Both are obviously working with the same material; but because of personal peculiarities they each see things from a different angle, and thus they evolve fundamentally different views and theories.[59]

Jung concluded that these "personal peculiarities" were in fact due to typological differences: Freud's system was predominantly extraverted, while Adler's was introverted.[60]

These fundamentally opposite attitude-types are found in both sexes and at all levels of society. They are not a matter of conscious

---

[59] "The Problem of the Attitude-Type," *Two Essays,* CW 7, pars. 56f.

[60] Interestingly, von Franz distinguishes between Freud's psychological system and his personal typology. Freud himself, she believes, was an introverted feeling type, "and therefore his writings bear the characteristics of his inferior extraverted thinking." (Von Franz and James Hillman, *Jung's Typology,* p. 49)

choice or inheritance or education. Their occurrence is a general phenomenon having an apparently random distribution.

Two children in the same family are often of opposite types. "Ultimately," writes Jung, "it must be the individual disposition which decides whether [one] will belong to this or that type."[61] In fact, he believed the type antithesis was due to some unconscious, instinctive cause, for which there was likely a biological foundation:

> There are in nature two fundamentally different modes of adaptation which ensure the continued existence of the living organism. The one consists in a high rate of fertility, with low powers of defence and short duration of life for the single individual; the other consists in equipping the individual with numerous means of self-preservation plus a low fertility rate. . . . [Similarly] the peculiar nature of the extravert constantly urges him to expend and propagate himself in every way, while the tendency of the introvert is to defend himself against all demands from outside, to conserve his energy by withdrawing it from objects, thereby consolidating his own position.[62]

While it is apparent that some individuals have a greater capacity, or disposition, to adapt to life in one way or another, it is not known why. Jung suspected there might be physiological causes of which we have as yet no knowledge, since a reversal or distortion of type often proves harmful to one's physical well-being.

No one, of course, is only introverted or extraverted. Although each of us, in the process of following our dominant inclination or adapting to our immediate world, invariably develops one attitude more than the other, the opposite attitude is still potentially there.

Indeed, familial circumstances may force one at an early age to take on an attitude that is not natural, thus violating the individual's innate disposition. "As a rule," writes Jung, "whenever such a falsification of type takes place . . . the individual becomes neurotic later, and can be cured only by developing the attitude consonant

---

[61] *Psychological Types,* CW 6, par. 560.

[62] Ibid., par. 559.

with his nature."[63]

This certainly complicates the type issue, since everyone is more or less neurotic—that is, one-sided.

In general, the introvert is simply unconscious of his or her extraverted side, because of an habitual orientation toward the inner world. The extravert's introversion is similarly dormant and may eventually emerge, given favorable circumstances.

In fact, the undeveloped attitude becomes an aspect of the shadow—all those things about ourselves we are not conscious of, our unrealized potential, our "unlived life." Moreover, being unconscious, when the inferior attitude surfaces—that is, when the introvert's extraversion, or the extravert's introversion, is constellated (activated)—it will tend to do so, just like the inferior function, in an emotional, socially unadapted way.

Since what is of value to the introvert is the opposite of what is important to the extravert, the inferior attitude regularly bedevils one's relationships with others.

To illustrate this, Jung tells the anecdotal story of two youths, one an introverted type, the other extraverted, rambling in the countryside.[64] They come upon a castle. Both want to visit it, but for different reasons. The introvert wonders what it's like inside; the extravert is game for adventure.

At the gate the introvert draws back. "Perhaps we aren't allowed in," he says—imagining guard dogs, policemen and fines in the background. The extravert is undeterred. "Oh, they'll let us in all right," he says—with visions of kindly old watchmen and the possibility of meeting an attractive girl.

On the strength of extraverted optimism, the two finally get inside the castle. There they find some dusty rooms with a collection of old manuscripts. As it happens, old manuscripts are the main interest of the introvert. He whoops with joy and enthusiastically peruses the treasures. He talks to the caretaker, asks for the curator,

---

[63] Ibid., par. 560.
[64] See "The Problem of the Attitude-Type," *Two Essays,* CW 7, pars. 81ff.

becomes quite animated; his shyness has vanished, objects have taken on a seductive glamour.

Meanwhile, the spirits of the extravert have fallen. He becomes glum, begins to yawn. There are no kindly watchmen, no pretty girls, just an old castle made into a museum. The manuscripts remind him of a library, libraries are associated with university, university with studies and examinations. He finds the whole thing incredibly boring.

"Isn't it marvelous," cries the introvert, "look at these!"—to which the extravert replies grumpily, "Nothing here for me, let's go." This annoys the introvert, who secretly swears never again to go rambling with an inconsiderate extravert. The latter is completely frustrated and now can think of nothing but that he'd rather be out of doors on a lovely spring day.

Jung points out that the two youths are wandering together in happy symbiosis until they come upon the castle. They enjoy a degree of harmony because they are collectively adapted to each other; the natural attitude of the one complements the natural attitude of the other.

The introvert is curious but hesitant; the extravert opens the door. But once inside, the types invert themselves: the former becomes fascinated by the object, the latter by his negative thoughts. The introvert now cannot be induced to go out and the extravert regrets ever setting foot inside.

What has happened? The introvert has become extraverted and the extravert introverted. But the opposite attitude of each manifests in a socially inferior way: the introvert, overpowered by the object, does not appreciate that his friend is bored; the extravert, disappointed in his expectations of romantic adventure, becomes moody and sullen, and doesn't care about his friend's excitement.

This is a simple example of the way in which the inferior attitude is autonomous. What we are not conscious of in ourselves is by definition beyond our control. When the undeveloped attitude is constellated, we are prey to all kinds of disruptive emotions—in a word, we are "complexed."

In the above story the two youths could be called shadow brothers. In relationships between men and women, the psychological dynamics are better understood through Jung's concept of the contrasexual archetypes: anima—a man's inner image of a woman—and animus—a woman's inner image of a man.[65]

In general, the extraverted man has an introverted anima, while the introverted woman has an extraverted animus, and vice versa. This picture can change through psychological work on oneself, but these inner images are commonly projected onto persons of the opposite sex, with the result that either attitude-type is prone to marry its opposite. This is likely to happen because each type is unconsciously complementary to the other.

Recall that the introvert is inclined to be reflective, to think things out and consider carefully before acting. Shyness and a degree of distrust of objects results in hesitation and some difficulty in adapting to the external world. The extravert, on the other hand, being attracted to the outer world, is fascinated by new and unknown situations. As a general rule the extravert acts first and thinks afterward; action is swift and not subject to misgivings or hesitation.

"The two types," writes Jung, "therefore seem created for a symbiosis. The one takes care of reflection and the other sees to the initiative and practical action. When the two types marry they may effect an ideal union."[66]

Discussing such a typical situation, Jung points out that it is ideal only so long as the partners are occupied with their adaptation to "the manifold external needs of life":

> But when . . . external necessity no longer presses, then they have time to occupy themselves with one another. Hitherto they stood back to back and defended themselves against necessity. But now

---

[65] See "The Syzygy: Anima and Animus," *Aion,* CW 9ii.

[66] "The Problem of the Attitude-Type," *Two Essays,* CW 7, par. 80.

they turn face to face and look for understanding—only to discover that they have never understood one another. Each speaks a different language. Then the conflict between the two types begins. This struggle is envenomed, brutal, full of mutual depreciation, even when conducted quietly and in the greatest intimacy. For the value of the one is the negation of value for the other.[67]

Fortunately, in the course of life we are generally obliged to develop both introversion and extraversion to some extent. This is necessary not only in order to coexist with others, but also for the development of individual character. "We cannot in the long run," writes Jung, "allow one part of our personality to be cared for symbiotically by another."[68] Yet that is in effect what is happening when we rely on friends, relatives or lovers to carry our inferior attitude or function.

If the inferior attitude is not consciously allowed some expression in our lives, we are likely to become bored and boring, uninteresting to both ourselves and others. And since there is energy tied up with whatever in ourselves is unconscious, we will not have the zest for life that goes with a well-balanced personality.

It is important to realize, again, that a person's activities are not always a reliable indication of the attitude-type. The life of the party may indeed be an extravert, but not necessarily. Similarly, long periods of solitude do not automatically mean that one is an introvert. The party-goer may be an introvert living out his shadow; the solitaire may be an extravert who has simply run out of steam, or has been forced by circumstances to be alone. In other words, while a particular activity may be associated with introversion or extraversion, this does not so easily translate into the type one is.

The crucial factor in determining type, as opposed to simply which attitude is currently prominent, is therefore not what one does but rather the motivation for doing it—*the direction in which one's energy naturally, and usually, flows:* for the extravert the ob-

---

[67] Ibid.
[68] Ibid., par. 86.

ject is interesting and attractive, while the subject, or psychic reality, is more important to the introvert.

The great difficulty in determining anyone's typology, especially one's own, is due to the fact that the dominant conscious attitude is unconsciously compensated or balanced by its opposite.

Introversion or extraversion, as a typical attitude, indicates an essential bias that conditions one's whole psychic process. The habitual mode of reaction determines not only the style of behavior, but also the quality of subjective experience. Moreover, it determines what is required in terms of compensation by the unconscious. Since either attitude is by itself one-sided, there would be a complete loss of psychic balance if there were no compensation by an unconscious counterposition.

Hence alongside or behind the introvert's usual way of functioning there is an unconscious extraverted attitude that automatically compensates the one-sidedness of consciousness. Similarly, the one-sidedness of extraversion is balanced or modified by an unconscious introverted attitude.

Strictly speaking, there is no demonstrable "attitude of the unconscious," but only ways of functioning that are colored by unconsciousness. It is in this sense that one can speak of a compensating attitude in the unconscious.

As we have seen, generally only one of the four functions is differentiated enough to be freely manipulable by the conscious will. The others are wholly or partially unconscious, and the inferior function mostly so. Thus the conscious orientation of the thinking type is balanced by unconscious feeling, and vice versa, while sensation is compensated by intuition, and so on.

Jung speaks of a "numinal accent" that falls on either the object or the subject, depending on whether one is extraverted or introverted. This numinal accent also "selects" one or other of the four functions, whose differentiation is essentially an empirical consequence of typical differences in the functional attitude.[69] Thus one

---

[69] *Psychological Types,* CW 6, pars. 982ff.

finds extraverted feeling in an introverted intellectual, introverted sensation in an extraverted intuitive, and so on.

An additional problem in establishing a person's typology is that unconscious, undifferentiated functions can color a personality to such an extent that an outside observer might easily mistake one type for another. For instance, the rational types (thinking and feeling) will have relatively inferior irrational functions (sensation and intuition), so that what they consciously and intentionally do may accord with reason (from their own point of view), but their actions may well be characterized by infantile, primitive sensations and intuitions. As Jung points out,

> Since there are vast numbers of people whose lives consist more of what happens to them than of actions governed by rational intentions, [an onlooker], after observing them closely, might easily describe both [thinking and feeling types] as irrational. And one has to admit that only too often a man's unconscious makes a far stronger impression on an observer than his consciousness does, and that his actions are of considerably more importance than his rational intentions.[70]

Indeed, it can be as difficult to establish one's own type as that of another person, especially when people have already become bored with their primary function and dominant attitude. Von Franz comments:

> They very often assure you with absolute sincerity that they belong to the type opposite from what they really are. The extravert swears that he is deeply introverted, and vice versa. This comes from the fact that the inferior function subjectively feels itself to be the real one, it feels itself the more important, more genuine attitude. . . . It does no good, therefore, to think of what matters most when trying to discover one's type; rather ask: "What do I habitually do most?"[71]

In practice, it is often helpful to ask oneself: What is my greatest cross? From what do I suffer the most? Where is it in life that I al-

---

[70] Ibid., par. 602.
[71] "The Inferior Function," in von Franz and Hillman, *Jung's Typology,* pp. 19ff.

ways knock my head against the wall and feel foolish? The answers to such questions generally lead to the inferior attitude and function, which then, with some determination and a good deal of patience, may perhaps be brought to a degree of consciousness.

*

Jung's model of typology is based on preferential or habitual ways of functioning. Used responsibly, it is a valuable guide to our dominant psychological disposition, the way we mostly are. It also reveals, by inference, the way we mostly *aren't*—but could also be.

Where, then, is the rest of us (mostly)?

Theoretically, we can say that the inferior or undeveloped attitude and functions are part of that side of ourselves Jung called the shadow. The reason for this is both conceptual and pragmatic.

Conceptually, the shadow, like the ego, is a complex. But where the ego, as the dominant complex of consciousness, is associated with aspects of oneself that are more or less known (as "I"), the shadow is comprised of personality characteristics that are not part of one's usual way of being in the world, and therefore more or less alien to one's sense of personal identity. Hence it is commonly projected onto others.

The shadow is potentially both creative and destructive: creative in that it represents aspects of oneself that have been buried or that might yet be realized; destructive in the sense that its value system and motivations tend to undermine or disturb one's conscious image of oneself, the so-called persona.

The shadow, then, can both destroy life and bestow it. The broker who embezzles, the priest who toys with choir boys, the husband who philanders, the wife who sleeps with another man, such as these have an opportunity to become more aware of who they really are. Besieged by desires, and confronted by actions, incompatible with the persona, they may reject them in favor of an inauthentic life, or acknowledge and assimilate them to their greater consciousness. The outside world may not know of their struggles, but everyone knows character when they experience it in another.

The assimilation of the shadow is indeed the making of a man or woman. The shadow can tax our conscience by not giving a damn for collective values. It may upset our lives by demanding our attention, our acceptance.

I think of Victor, a married eighty-year-old Anglican priest who for thirty years had an ongoing love affair with a married parishioner. No one is much surprised by such things these days, given the generally low esteem accorded the priesthood, and of course extramarital affairs are too ubiquitous to raise an eyebrow, but I learned much from this man. I learned that a person of substantial moral fiber could with insight and personal integrity come to accommodate his shadow, actually live it out, without falling apart from guilt. And for five years I did nothing except listen to his conflicts without judgment and encourage him to hold the tension. He was a hero in my eyes, and I told him so. And he was unassuming enough not to become inflated. I knew too a 60ish love-struck woman in the same boat who swore that the continuing tension gave her life meaning.

These folks are not unique. I dare say there are many other such unsung heroes and heroines out there who have learned to accept and live guiltlessly with their other sides, often with no analysis or high-falutin' learning at all. Call it immoral, perhaps, or unconventional, but not inauthentic or unethical after reading chapter ten here in Book Two: "A Psychological View of Conscience."

Everything that is not ego is relatively unconscious. Indeed, before the contents of the unconscious have been differentiated, the shadow *is* the unconscious. Since the opposite attitude and the inferior functions are by definition relatively unconscious, they are naturally tied up with the shadow.

In one's immediate world, there are attitudes and behavior that are socially acceptable, and those that are not. In our formative years it is natural to repress, or suppress, unacceptable aspects of ourselves. They "fall into" the shadow. What is left is the persona—the "I" one presents to the outside world.

The persona would live up to what is expected, what is "proper." It is both a useful bridge socially and an indispensable protective covering. Without a persona, we are simply too vulnerable. We regularly cover up our inferiorities with a persona, since we do not like our weaknesses to be seen. (The introverted thinking type at a noisy party may grit his teeth but smile. The extraverted feeling type may pretend to be studying when she is really climbing the wall for lack of company.)

Civilized society, life as we more or less know it, depends on interactions between people through the persona. But it is psychologically unhealthy to identify with it, to believe that we are simply the person we show to others.

Generally speaking, the shadow is less civilized, more primitive, cares little for social propriety. What is of value to the persona is anathema to the shadow, and vice versa. Hence the shadow and the persona function in a compensatory way: the brighter the light, the darker the shadow. The more one identifies with the persona—which in effect is to deny that one has a shadow—the more trouble one will have with the unacknowledged areas of the personality.

Thus the shadow constantly challenges the morality of the persona, and, to the extent that ego-consciousness identifies with the persona, the shadow also threatens the ego. In the process of psychological development that Jung called individuation, disidentification from the persona and the conscious assimilation of the shadow go hand in hand. The ideal is to have an ego strong enough to acknowledge both persona and shadow without identifying with either of them.

This is not as easy as it sounds. We tend to identify with what we are good at, and why shouldn't we? The superior function, after all, has an undeniable utilitarian value. It greases the wheels; life runs smoothly. The superior function generally brings praise, material rewards, a degree of satisfaction. It inevitably becomes a prominent aspect of the persona. Why give it up? The answer is that we don't—unless we have to. And when do we "have to"?—when we encounter situations in life that are not amenable to the way we usually function; that is, when the way we habitually tend to look at things no longer works. Then, welcome to midlife crisis (at any age)—and the chance to become more conscious.

In practice, as noted earlier, the shadow and everything associated with it is virtually synonymous with unlived life. "There is more to life than this," is a remark heard often in the consulting room. All that I consciously am and aspire to be effectively shuts out what I might be, could be, *also am.* Some of what I "also am" has been or is repressed because it was—or is—socially or professionally unacceptable; some is simply unrealized potential.

Through introspection, we can become aware of shadow aspects of the personality, but we may still resist them or fear their influence. And even where they are known and would be welcome, they are not readily available to the conscious will. For instance, though I may be well aware that my intuition is shadowy—primitive and unadapted—that knowledge is not enough to allow me to call it up when it's needed. I may know that feeling is required in a particular situation but for the life of me can't muster it. I want to enjoy the party but my carefree extraverted side has vanished. I may know I'm due for some solitary introversion, but the lure of the bright lights is just too strong.

The shadow does not necessarily require equal time with the ego, but for a balanced personality it does need recognition. For the introvert this may involve an occasional night on the town— against one's "better judgment." For the extravert it might involve—in spite of oneself—an evening staring at the wall. In general, the person whose shadow is dormant gives the impression of being artificial, forced. Typologically, this works both ways: the extravert seems to lack depth; the introvert appears socially inept.

The introvert's psychological situation is laid bare in Franz Kafka's observation:

> Whoever leads a solitary life and yet now and then wants to attach
> himself somewhere; whoever, according to changes in the time of

day, the weather, the state of his business and the like, suddenly wishes to see any arm at all to which he might cling—he will not be able to manage for long without a window looking on to the street.[72]

Similarly, the extravert may only become conscious of the shadow when struck by the vacuity of social intercourse.

There is a balance between introversion and extraversion, as there is between the normally opposing functions, but it rarely becomes necessary—or even possible—to seek it out, until and unless the conscious ego-personality falls on its face.

In that case, which happily manifests as a nervous breakdown rather than a more serious psychotic break, the shadow side demands to be recognized. The resulting turmoil may upset one's life and disturb many things one has known or believed about oneself, but it has the advantage of overcoming the tyranny of the dominant attitude of consciousness. If the symptoms are then attended to with some seriousness, the whole personality can be enlivened.

There is by definition a natural conflict between ego and shadow, but when one has made a commitment to live out as much of one's potential as possible, then the integration of the shadow— including the inferior attitude and functions—from being merely theoretically desirable, becomes a practical necessity. Hence the process of assimilating the shadow requires the capacity to live with some psychological tension and uncertainty.

The introverted man, for instance, under the influence of his inferior extraverted shadow, is prone to imagine he is missing something: vivacious women, fast company, excitement. He himself may see these as chimeras, but his shadow yearns for them. His shadow will lead him into the darkest venues, and then, as often as not (whimsically), abandon him. What is left? A lonely introvert who longs for home.

On the other hand, the extraverting introvert who is taken at face value—as a true extravert—is liable to end up in hot water.

---

[72] "The Street Window," in *The Penal Colony: Stories and Short Pieces,* p. 39.

Whereas the introverting extravert has only himself to deal with, the extraverting introvert often makes a tremendous impact on those who cross his path, but he might not want to be with them the next day. When his introversion asserts itself, he may literally want nothing to do with other people. Thus the introverted intellectual whose shadow is a charming, carefree Don Juan wreaks havoc on the hearts of unsuspecting women.

True extraverts genuinely enjoy being part of the crowd. That is their natural home. They are restless alone, not because they are avoiding themselves, but because their sense of self is clarified and confirmed by relationship with others. The introverted shadow of extraverts may encourage them to stay home and find out who they really are. But just as introverts may be abandoned by their shadows in a noisy bar, so extraverts may be left high and dry—and lonely— when on their own.

The opposite attitude and the inferior functions regularly appear as shadow figures in dreams and fantasies. According to Jung's understanding, all the characters that appear in dreams are personifications of aspects of the dreamer.[73] Dream activity becomes heightened when a function not usually available to consciousness is required. Thus, for instance, a man who is a thinking type, after a quarrel with his wife, may be assailed in his dreams by images of primitive feeling persons, dramatically illustrating a side of himself he needs to acknowledge. Similarly, the sensation type stuck in a rut may be confronted in dreams by an intuitive type showing some possible ways out, and so on.

To assimilate a function means to live with it in the foreground of consciousness. "If one does a little cooking or sewing," writes von Franz, "it does not mean that the sensation function has been assimilated":

> Assimilation means that the whole adaptation of conscious life, for a

---

[73] See "General Aspects of Dream Psychology," and "On the Nature of Dreams," *The Structure and Dynamics of the Psyche*, CW 8.

while, lies on that one function. Switching over to an auxiliary function takes place when one feels that the present way of living has become lifeless, when one gets more or less constantly bored with oneself and one's activities. . . . The best way to know how to switch is simply to say, "All right, all this is now completely boring, it does not mean anything to me any more. Where in my past life is an activity that I feel I could still enjoy? An activity out of which I could still get a kick?" If a person then genuinely picks up that activity, he will see that he has switched over to another function.[74]

—and, to some extent, assimilated an aspect of the shadow that was previously inaccessible.

*

The final word here must be that aside from the clinical implications of Jung's model of typology (of which there are too many to explore here),[75] its major importance continues to be the perspective it offers on oneself.

Using Jung's model in a personally meaningful way requires the same kind of dedicated reflection as does getting a handle on one's shadow and any of the other complexes. In other words, it involves paying close attention, over an extended period of time, to where one's energy tends to go, the motivations that lie behind one's behavior, and the problems that arise in relationships with others.

Modern technology has provided us with many useful tools, quick and easy ways to accomplish what would otherwise be onerous or time-consuming tasks. The process of understanding oneself, however, is not amenable to short cuts. It remains inextricably linked to, and enriched by, individual effort.

*

It was just around this point in the writing of this book that I took

---

[74] "The Inferior Function," in von Franz and Hillman, *Jung's Typology*, p. 59.

[75] See H.K. Fierz, "The Clinical Significance of Extraversion and Introversion," in my *Personality Types: Jung's Model of Typology*, pp. 101ff.

a tumble. Literally. I imagine I was abducted by aliens and taken to their Mother Ship where they hammered on my ankle until it fractured and shredded ligaments—perhaps in the spirit of scientific enquiry: how much pain can an Earthling endure?

In truth, I remember only exiting my hot tub and suddenly finding myself on the floor in agony. Well, that's the way of aliens—they can wipe out your memory as well as your bones. It took me some hours to crawl to a telephone and call for help.

Of course, in accordance with the principle of Occam's Razor, there were no aliens involved at all, only my inattention.[76]

In any case, attuned as I am to the ubiquity of synchronicity, I am obliged to ask myself if this was simply an accident or a "meaningful coincidence"—the conjunction in time of inner and outer phenomena, and if the latter, what purpose did it serve in terms of my individuation?[77]

Well, it certainly slowed me down, necessitating many painful weeks in hospital and rehab, which effectively put my productive life on hold. As well, once home, being confined to quarters by necessity accorded with my natural inclination to stay put. In that light, being immobilized may be considered, like Adam's seduction by Eve, a *felix culpa,* a fortunate happening,

---

[76] Occam's razor (sometimes spelled Ockham's razor) is a principle attributed to the fourteenth-century English logician and Franciscan friar William of Ockham. The principle states that the explanation of any phenomenon should make as few assumptions as possible, eliminating, or "shaving off," those that make no difference in the observable predictions of the explanatory hypothesis or theory. The principle is often expressed in Latin as the *lex parsimoniae* ("law of parsimony" or "law of succinctness"). Jung refers to this principle as *not* being abrogated simply because the existence of more than one psychological type has to be assumed in order satisfactorily to understand the "type problem." ("The Type Problem in Classical and Medieval Thought," *Psychological Types,* CW 6, par. 61).

[77] The phenomenon of synchronicity occurs when there is a meaningful coincidence between an inner psychological state or mood and an outer happening. And the determination of whether the congruence is meaningful or not is entirely subjective. That is why synchronicity cannot be proven or demonstrated scientifically—it can't be repeated objectively in a laboratory. It can only be experienced. See my book *Jungian Psychology Unplugged* and Sparks, *At the Heart of Matter.*

The possibilities are many, but one thing is sure—the unconscious is always waiting to give you a spill.

Anyway, I will manage, drawing on Stoic reserves and millenniums of primordial patience.

7
The Problem of the Attitude-Type
(from *Two Essays on Analytical Psychology,*
CW 7; vintage 1917/1943)

Freud's theory espoused Eros, Adler's the will to power. Logically, the opposite of love is hate, and of Eros, Phobos (fear); but psychologically it is the will to power. Where love reigns, there is no will to power; and where the will to power is paramount, love is lacking. The one is but the shadow of the other.[78]

"The Problem of the Attitude-Type" is primarily concerned with differentiating the psychological approaches to neurosis espoused by Freud and Alfred Adler and Jung himself. Indeed, Jung's reflections resulted in his model of typology, as summarized here in the previous chapter.

Jung begins this essay by outlining the opposing views of neurosis proposed by Freud and Adler. Freud believed that the source of neuroses was disturbances in infant and childhood sexuality. Adler traced adult neurotic behavior to the powerlessness experienced in childhood. Jung saw both of these hypotheses as reductive and possibly relevant in particular cases, but inadequate to explain the generality of neuroses as he encountered them among both men and women in his psychiatric practice—and in himself.

Referring to the "mad and monstrous devastation, a mass murder without parallel" that characterized the First World War, Jung sums up his view that Adler's approach, based as it is on rational intentions, is wholly inadequate in dealing with the irrationality of fate:

What is true of humanity in general is also true of each individual, for humanity consists only of individuals. And as is the psychology of humanity so also is the psychology of the individual. The World

---

[78] "The Problem of the Attitude-Type," *Two Essays,* CW 7, par. 78.

War brought a terrible reckoning with the rational intentions of civilization. What is called "will" in the individual is called "imperialism" in nations; for all will is a demonstration of power over fate, i.e., the exclusion of chance. Civilization is the rational "purposeful" sublimation of free energies, brought about by will and intention. It is the same with the individual, and just as the idea of a world civilization received a fearful correction at the hands of war, so the individual must often learn in his life that so-called "disposable" energies are not his to dispose.[79]

Jung goes on then to consider the irrationality of life and the vexing question of disposable energy:

Psychic energy is a very fastidious thing which insists on fulfilment of its conditions. However much energy may be present, we cannot make it serviceable until we have succeeded in finding the right gradient.[80]

As illustration, Jung tells of a self-made American business man who consulted him two years after retiring. This man had purchased a splendid estate on which he planned to live a life of leisure, enjoying horses, automobiles, golf, tennis, women, parties, and the like. Alas, things did not work out as hoped, for "he had reckoned without his host."

The energy which should have been at his disposal would not enter into these alluring prospects, but went capering off in quite another direction. A few weeks after the initiation of the longed-for life of bliss, he began brooding over peculiar, vague sensations in his body, and a few weeks more sufficed to plunge him into a state of extreme hypochondria. He had a complete nervous collapse. From a healthy man of uncommon physical strength and abounding energy, he became a peevish child.[81]

The man saw medical specialists who pronounced him physi-

---

[79] Ibid., par. 74.
[80] Ibid., par. 76.
[81] Ibid., par. 75.

cally fit. But nothing availed. One doctor advised him to go back to work, but he could not reclaim his former interest in the business world. His hypochondria persisted and when Jung saw him he had already become "a hopeless moral ruin."

> I tried to make clear to him that though such colossal energy might be withdrawn from the business, the question remained, where should it go? The finest horses, the fastest cars, and the most amusing parties may very likely fail to allure the energy, although it would be rational enough to think that a man who had devoted his whole life to serious work had a sort of natural right to enjoy himself. Yes, if fate behaved in a humanly rational way, it would certainly be so; first work, then well-earned rest. But fate behaves irrationally, and the energy of life inconveniently demands a gradient agreeable to itself; otherwise it simply gets dammed up and turns destructive. . . . The ultimate goal was to drive him back, as it were, into his own body, after he had lived since his youth only in his head. He had differentiated one side of his being, the other side remained in an inert physical state. He would have needed this other side in order to live. The hypochondriacal "depression" pushed him down into the body he had always overlooked.[82]

The "host" this man had not reckoned with was apparently his unconscious and his body. The road to salvation, suggests Jung, would have been to explore his depression and the attendant fantasies, but this did not happen. "A case so far advanced," laments Jung, "can only be cared for until death; it can hardly be cured."

Jung also cites the case of a young married woman who developed neurotic symptoms (nervous asthma, anxiety, nightmares, crying fits, etc.), which were eventually traced to her feelings for a young Italian who had frightened her with a lustful look some years before her marriage. She was also distraught with grief over the sudden accidental death of her beloved father (on whose face she had once glimpsed a similar look), together with the discovery that her husband had developed a tender interest in another woman.

---

[82] Ibid.

Jung gives a brief account of the course of her analysis, culminating in an awareness of her repressed sexual feelings for her father and the need to discover a satisfactory outlet for her new-found disposable energy.

> In accordance with the psychological type of the patient, it would be rational to transfer the energy to an object—to philanthropic work, for example, or some useful activity. With exceptionally energetic natures that are not afraid of wearing themselves to the bone, if need be, or with people who delight in the toil and moil of such activities, this way is possible, but mostly it is impossible. For—do not forget—the libido, as this psychic energy is technically called, already possesses its object unconsciously, in the form of the young Italian or some equally real human substitute. In these circumstances sublimation is as impossible as it is desirable, because the real object generally offers the energy a much better gradient than do the most admirable ethical activities.[83]

Now enters the phenomenon of transference:

> It is unhappily the case that no man can direct the so-called disposable energy at will. It follows its own gradient. Indeed, it had already found that gradient even before we set the energy free from the unserviceable form to which it was linked. For we discover that the patient's fantasies, previously occupied with the young Italian, have now transferred themselves to the doctor. The doctor has himself become the object of the unconscious libido.[84]

Jung does not reveal whether this woman was a patient of his, but he points out that in such a case a resolution is finally possible only if "the doctor" can accept the erotic transference and all the projected infantile fantasies that inevitably accompany it. He ends::

> Once more, we shall put our trust in nature, hoping that, even before it is sought, an object will have been chosen which will provide a favourable gradient.[85]

---

[83] Ibid., par. 93.

[84] Ibid., par. 94.

[85] Ibid., par. 96.

Analysis, by unearthing troublesome unconscious contents, has the effect of releasing energy. But where that energy will go is as often as not a moral issue that taxes one's values and fortitude. And yet, along the way, it may also forge character.

Let us return now to the problematic issue of the attitude-type. In the previous chapter, I recounted Jung's story about what might happen when two youths, one introverted and the other extraverted, chance upon a castle. Here I want to emphasize his views on how such typological differences may contribute to discord between the sexes, since either type has a predilection to marry its opposite, each being complementary to the other.

In the castle story the two youths could be called shadow brothers. In relationships between men and women, the psychological dynamics are better understood through Jung's concept of the contrasexual archetypes: anima—a man's inner image of a woman—and animus—a woman's inner image of a man.

In general, the extraverted man has an introverted anima, while the introverted woman has an extraverted animus, and vice versa. This picture can change through psychological work on oneself, but these inner images are commonly projected onto persons of the opposite sex, with the result that either attitude-type is prone to marry its opposite. This is likely to happen because each type is unconsciously complementary to the other.

Recall that the introvert is inclined to be reflective, to think things out and consider carefully before acting. Shyness and a degree of distrust of objects results in hesitation and some difficulty in adapting to the external world. The extravert, on the other hand, being attracted to the outer world, is fascinated by new and unknown situations. As a general rule the extravert acts first and thinks afterward; action is swift and not subject to misgivings or hesitation.

The difficulties that regularly arise between different attitude-types are legion. In the previous chapter I quoted Jung's observation that what initially seems to be an ideal union may in time become uneasy and embittered.[86]

One might think that an understanding of typology would forestall such enmity and allow two people to live in peace, each acknowledging and appreciating the value of the other, but the reality is that even many individuals who have a good grasp on their psychological make-up may find it difficult or even impossible to tolerate an intimate relationship with someone of a different attitudinal orientation. Hence so many acrimonious divorces and separations.

*

I read in the newspaper today that we are essentially only empty vessels:

> Atoms are 99.9 percent empty space. If all the space was sucked out of the atoms in your body, you would shrink to the size of a grain of salt.[87]

That is an interesting perspective. On the other hand, I have it from the aliens that even a grain of salt, when filled with enough consciousness, can change the world.

---

[86] See above, p. 70.

[87] From *Focus Magazine* (U.K.), in Michael Kesterton, "Social Studies, a Daily Miscellany of Information," (*Globe and Mail,* Toronto, 26 July, 2007).

8
The Transcendent Function

(from *The Structure and Dynamics of the Psyche*, CW 8;
vintage 1916/1958)

Civilized life today demands concentrated, directed conscious functioning, and this entails the risk of a considerable dissociation from
the unconscious. The further we are able to remove ourselves from
the unconscious through directed functioning, the more readily a
powerful counter-position can build up in the unconscious, and
when this breaks out it may have disagreeable consequences.[88]

The tendencies of the conscious and the unconscious are the two
factors that together make up the transcendent function. It is called
"transcendent" because it makes the transition from one attitude to
another organically possible, without loss of the unconscious.[89]

The transcendent function may be one of Jung's most difficult concepts to understand, yet it is certainly one of the most important in
dealing with the ongoing problem of how one comes to terms with
the unconscious.[90] It is also one of the earliest indications that Jung
was not satisfied with Freud's notion of libido as exclusively sexual
energy.

Perhaps it is necessary first to dispel the idea that "transcendent"
refers to some other-worldly "beyond," a mystical or spiritual
realm, which is the common and proper concern of theology and

---

[88] "The Transcendent Function," *The Structure and Dynamics of the Psyche*, CW
8, par. 139.

[89] Ibid., par. 145.

[90] Although this essay was originally written in 1916 when Jung was forty-one, for
years it lay forgotten in Jung's files, finally coming to light in 1953. It was first
published in 1957 in an English translation by the English medical doctor Richard
Pope, one of the first graduates of the Zurich Jung Institute (founded in 1948).
Jung himself revised it for publication in German in 1958, which version was later
translated for inclusion in the *Collected Works*.

religious philosophy. As Jung clarifies in a prefatory note:

> There is nothing mysterious or metaphysical about the term "transcendent function." It means a psychological function comparable in its way to a mathematical function of the same name, which is a function of real and imaginary numbers. The psychological "transcendent function" arises from the union of conscious and unconscious contents.[91]

In short, the transcendent function is a phenomenon that bridges or reconciles opposing points of view.

Jung realized early on in his clinical practice that there was a marked disparity between the contents of ego-consciousness and the unconscious. This lack of congruence, he discovered, was purposeful and due to the fact that the unconscious behaves in a compensatory or complementary manner toward consciousness. There are several reasons for this:

1. The contents of consciousness must have attained a certain degree of energic intensity; otherwise they would have remained in the unconscious.

2. Because of the directed manner in which consciousness functions, material incompatible with the conscious attitude is inhibited and sinks into the unconscious.

3. Consciousness is based on what is momentarily necessary for adaptation, whereas the unconscious contains not only forgotten material from a person's own individual past, but all the inherited behavior patterns that constitute the structure of the human mind, namely the archetypes.

4. And finally, the unconscious contains all the fantasy material that lacks the intensity to cross the threshold of consciousness, but which in the course of time and under suitable conditions may become conscious.

---

[91] "The Transcendent Function," *The Structure and Dynamics of the Psyche,* CW 8, par. 131.

The disparity between consciousness and the unconscious is notable because it usually manifests as conflict. Although healthy in the long run, conflict gives the ego a hard time in terms of uncertainty and indecision. This regularly happens when the unconscious, in the service of balancing psychic energies and/or seeking expression of the individual's unlived potential, prompts the ego to new directions and the ego resists.

It is natural and necessary for the ego to resist change, for its very one-sidedness is so useful for the successful accomplishment of day-to-day tasks. Without the continuity and reliability of directed thinking, science and technology, business, sports and leisure, and indeed civilization as we know it, would be impossible.

Still, the one-sidedness of ego-consciousness entails a certain disadvantage, for it inhibits or excludes all those psychic processes or elements that appear to be, or really are, incompatible with ego desires or needs. But how do we know, asks Jung, that certain psychic processes at work in the unconscious are "incompatible"? He answers:

> We know it by an act of judgment which determines the direction of the path that is chosen and desired. This judgment is partial and prejudiced, since it chooses one particular possibility at the cost of all the others. The judgment in its turn is always based on experience, i.e., on what is already known. As a rule it is never based on what is new, what is still unknown, and what under certain conditions might considerably enrich the directed process. It is evident that it cannot be, for the very reason that the unconscious contents are excluded from consciousness.[92]

It is true that the unknown is always more or less frightening because it threatens the stability of the ego. Hence we are prone to imagine that the influence of the unconscious (from the shadow and other complexes) is deleterious and ought to be resisted. This is often so, but not necessarily, for ego-consciousness can get off-

---

[92] Ibid., par. 136.

track in terms of individuation—who and what a person is meant to be. It follows, then, thanks to the self-regulating nature of the psyche, that the ego is well advised to attend to the possibilities "voiced" by the unconscious via, for instance, dreams, fantasies and synchronistic events.

It is in the nature of the psyche that its two components, consciousness and the unconscious, compensate each other. This means that whatever the conscious attitude may be, its counterposition exists in the unconscious. This is a given in the practice of Jungian psychology, hence the analyst's every effort in the analytic process is oriented toward bringing to the surface unconscious contents and accepting them without fear or favor, without judgment. "Where does your energy want to go?" is the analyst's mantra to clients in a conflict situation. And the answer is not found by rolling the die on my desk whose six faces are stamped with these possibilities: "read; disco; love; sex; pub; TV," or in Al Pacino's advice in *The Scent of a Woman:* "When in doubt, make love."

Alas, the problem invariably goes much deeper and wider than that, demanding sacrifice and moral courage. It may involve leaving one's job or profession, one's family, one's country, or any number of potentially life-shattering changes. But just one minute here, what may be life-shattering may instead turn out to be life-enhancing, and that is the dilemma that can keep a person's life on hold or spinning like a top. How does one decide which way to jump? It puts me in mind of the medieval knight placed before two doors and told: "In one there is a beautiful maiden, in the other a hungry tiger. You choose

No matter how hard one works on the material at hand, dreams and so on, that is metaphorically what it comes down to in the end: The lady or the tiger? And how to tell one from the other anyway? Perhaps they are one and the same and it doesn't matter—and that's the point.

But Jung was concerned not only with his analysands' current difficulties, but also with how they might deal with future problems. Analysis is not a cure for all time. Something new is always coming up, demanding new adaptations, decisions and choices.

Recall Jung's question in the passage at the head of this chapter, "What kind of mental and moral attitude is it necessary to have towards the disturbing influences of the unconscious and how can it be conveyed to the patient?"

The answer was obvious to Jung: narrow the gap between consciousness and the unconscious. This is done by recognizing the significance of unconscious contents in compensating the one-sidedness of consciousness and taking this into account when making significant life decisions.

This viewpoint is at the heart of Jung's constructive or synthetic (also called purposive or energic) approach to neurosis and its attendant symptoms, or indeed any manifestation of psychological distress. Freud sought their cause; Jung was more interested in their purpose, reflecting his abiding, experiential belief in the self-regulating nature of the psyche.

Jung's view is not actually incompatible with the traditional psychoanalytic reductive view (also called causal or mechanistic), namely that psychological problems are primarily sexual in nature and stem from Oedipal conflicts in childhood. It is truer to say that the two views are complementary: Freud looked to the past for the cause of psychic discomfort in the present; Jung focused on the present with an eye to what was possible in the future.

Jung did not dispute Freudian theory that Oedipal fixations can manifest as neurosis in later life. He agreed that certain periods in life, and particularly infancy, often have a permanent and determining influence on the personality. He simply pointed out that this was an insufficient explanation for those cases in which there was no trace of neurosis until the time of the breakdown.

> If the fixation were indeed real [i.e., the primary cause] we should expect to find its influence constant; in other words, a neurosis lasting throughout life. This is obviously not the case. The psychological determination of a neurosis is only partly due to an early infan-

tile predisposition; it must be due to some cause in the present as well. And if we carefully examine the kind of infantile fantasies and occurrences to which the neurotic is attached, we shall be obliged to agree that there is nothing in them that is specifically neurotic. Normal individuals have pretty much the same inner and outer experiences, and may be attached to them to an astonishing degree without developing a neurosis.[93]

What, then, determines why one person has a psychological crisis while another, perhaps in equally difficult circumstances, does not? Jung did not pose or answer this question directly, but the implication of all his work is that the individual psyche knows both its limits and its potential. If the former are being exceeded, or the latter not realized, a breakdown occurs. The psyche itself acts to correct the situation, as if to counter the mantra, "If it's not broke, don't fix it," with the injunction: "It's broke, so I will make you fix it." The Self, our inner regulating center, is our personal Mr. Fix-It. Talk about omelettes! Fixing a life may involve breaking a lot more eggs than we thought

We often find ourselves in a conflict situation where there is no rational solution. This is the classic beginning of the process of individuation. The situation is *meant* to have no resolution: the unconscious wants the hopeless conflict in order to put ego-consciousness up against the wall, so that one has to realize that whatever one does is wrong, whichever way one decides is wrong. This is meant to knock out the superiority of the ego, which likes to act from the illusion that it is in charge and is responsible for making decisions. If one is ethical enough to suffer to the core, then generally, because of the insolubility of the conflict, the Self manifests. Call it grace, if so inclined, for that is what it feels like

This is more than an article of faith for me, because I have experienced it several times—the deep slough of despair, not knowing which way to turn, not knowing which door to choose. I held the tension until the right path became clear, but it was not my ego's

---

[93] "Psychoanalysis and Neurosis," *Freud and Psychoanalysis,* CW 4, par. 564.

doing. Jung was asked in 1960 if he believed in God." He harumphed, "I don't need to believe, I know!"[94] And so when asked if I believe in the Self, I must likewise affirm, "I know!" There are light years between what the ego takes on faith and what it knows from experiencing the reality of the psyche. This is not a religious belief, but belief in the mystery; that, in itself, is spiritual.

The conflict that many men experience between their love for a mate and their feelings for another woman is so ubiquitous that it is trite. But it is a perfect example of how the anima, in service of the Self, can manouver a man into a situation that requires him to take seriously his feelings, his inner woman, and by extension the reality of the psyche. Think of Dante's vision of Beatrice as his soul guide, but don't forget that he had first to go through Hell. Of course a woman may find herself in a similar situation, but in this case we say that her animus or inner man is involved in the disturbance.

To summarize the foregoing, Jung's belief was that in a psychological crisis unconscious contents are automatically activated in an attempt to compensate the one-sided, directed attitude of consciousness. This is in fact true at any age, but it is not usually necessary in the first half of life to deal with what we call the problem of opposites—the disparity between conscious ego-attitudes and what is going on in the unconscious

The problems of young people, notes Jung,

> generally come from a collision between the forces of reality and an inadequate, infantile attitude, which from the causal point of view is characterized by an abnormal dependence on the real or imaginary parents."[95].

Therapy with the young, therefore, usually involves transferring the imagos of the parents onto more suitable substitutes and encouraging the development of a strong ego. In later life, a strong but flexible ego is needed in order to survive a psychological crisis.

---

[94] "The 'Face to Face' Interview," in William McGuire and R.F.C. Hull, eds., *C.G. Jung Speaking: Interviews and Encounters*, p. 428.

[95] "The Problem of the Attitude-Type," *Two Essays*, CW 7, par. 88.

In "The Transcendent Function," Jung outlines virtually the only "technique" he ever advocated in the treatment of neuroses and the pursuit of wholeness. It is called active imagination, briefly described here in an earlier chapter, together with how I used it myself.[96]

Active imagination is difficult to teach, but it can be learned and in time it has the salutary result of freeing the analysand from dependence on the analyst as it manifests in the transference. And until the analysand has this tool, the analyst is obliged to mediate the transcendent function to his or her charges; that is, help them to bring consciousness and unconscious together and so arrive at a new attitude, which often as not appears as a symbol (a dream image or fantasy), with the symbol being understood not mechanistically, semiotically, as a sign for elementary instinct, but rather as "the best possible expression for a complex fact not yet clearly apprehended by consciousness."[97]

As an example of the transformation of energy and the difference between a sign and a symbol, Jung tells of the ceremonial spring ritual performed by an Australian tribe, the Wachandi:

> They dig a hole in the ground, oval in shape and set about with bushes so that it looks like a woman's genitals. Then they dance round that hole, holding their spears in front of them in imitation of an erect penis. As they dance round, they thrust their spears into the hole, shouting: "Pull nira, pulli nira, wataka!" (not a pit, not a pit, but a c___! During the ceremony none of the participants is allowed to look at a woman.[98]

Jung interprets:

> The Wachandi's hole in the earth is not a sign for the genitals of a woman, but a symbol that stands for the idea of the earth woman

---

[96] Above, pp. 14f.

[97] "The Transcendent Function," *The Structure and Dynamics of the Psyche,* CW 8, par. 148.

[98] "On Psychic Energy," Ibid., par. 83.

who is to be made fruitful. To mistake it for a human woman would be to interpret the symbol semiotically, and this would fatally disturb the value of the ceremony. It is for this reason that none of the dancers may look at a woman.[99]

The task in active imagination is to wrestle with the symbol until its meaning and purpose become clear to consciousness. That is the first step, and then:

> Once the unconscious content has been given form and the meaning of the formulation has been understood, the question arises as to how the ego will relate to this position, and how the ego and the unconscious are to come to terms, This is the second and more important stage of the procedure, the bringing together of opposites for the production of a third, the transcendent function, At this stage it is no longer the unconscious that takes the lead but the ego.[100]

And Jung warns:

> The position of the ego must be maintained as being of equal value to the counter-position of the unconscious, and vice versa, This amounts to a very necessary warning, for just as the conscious mind of civilized man has a restrictive effect on the unconscious, so the rediscovered unconscious often has a really dangerous effect on the ego.[101]

I have skirted an important question so far, but here it is, front and center: What is required to produce the transcendent function? What makes it happen?

Well, first of all, one needs the unconscious material. Dream images are a rich source of information if they are evaluated with an eye to how they might pertain to the current situation. Fantasies are another source, as are physical accidents, faux pas of any kind, and synchronistic events.

However, often there is no such material readily at hand. In such

---

[99] Ibid., par. 88.

[100] "The Transcendent Function," ibid., par. 181.

[101] Ibid. par. 183.

cases, one must resort to artificial aids, as it were, by giving the unconscious a voice through some expressive art or craft—writing, painting, modeling, knitting, dancing, etc. And here the natural starting point for producing the transcendent function is a mood one finds oneself in. Jung explains:

> *In the intensity of the emotional disturbance itself lies the value, the energy which he should have at his disposal in order to remedy the state of reduced adaptation*
>
> In order, therefore, to gain possession of the energy that is in the wrong place, he must make the emotional state the basis or starting point of the procedure. He must make himself as conscious as possible of the mood he is in, sinking himself in it without reserve and noting down on paper all the fantasies and other associations that come up. Fantasy must be allowed the freest possible play . . . . Out of this preoccupation with the object there comes a more or less complete expression of the mood, which reproduces the content of the depression in some way, either concretely or symbolically. . . . The whole procedure is a kind of enrichment and clarification of the affect, whereby the affect and its contents are brought nearer to consciousness, becoming at the same time more impressive and more understandable. . . .This is the beginning of the transcendent function, i.e., of the collaboration of conscious and unconscious data.[102]

It is not important for the product to be technically or aesthetically satisfying. The important thing is to allow the fantasy to have free play without criticism or judgment. Then the result embodies the striving of the unconscious for the light and the striving of ego-consciousness for substance. It is the transcendent function, the *tertium non datur,* the third not rationally given.

That is the activity Jung advised pursuing in order to come to terms with the unconscious and thus to profit from the tension that naturally exists between rational consciousness and the essentially irrational, instinctive, unconscious drives that can be so disturbing if not attended to. Naturally, this is possible only when the con-

---

[102] Ibid., pars. 166f. (emphasis in the original).

scious mind is motivated, as when it finds itself in a critical situation, faced with a choice between the metaphorical equivalents of lady and tiger.

Jung ends his peroration like this:

> In whatever form the opposites appear in the individual, at bottom it is always a matter of a consciousness lost and obstinately stuck in one-sidedness, confronted with the image of instinctive wholeness and freedom. This presents a picture of the anthropoid and archaic man . . . . who, compensating and correcting our one-sidedness, emerges from the darkness and shows us how and where we have deviated from the basic pattern and crippled ourselves psychically.[103].

The practice of active imagination can forestall an eruption of the unconscious, which may happen when its contents are repressed. No such eruption is pretty. Individual lives can be torn asunder by unheeded, unintegrated unconscious forces. This can also manifest on a collective level, which happened, for example, in the French Revolution, in Germany in the 1930s, and around the world during the so-called Cultural Revolution of the 1960s.

For the record, the chart opposite summarizes the typical progression of psychic events in a psychological crisis.

---

[103] Ibid., par. 190.

The Self-Regulation of the Psyche

1. Difficulty of adaptation. Difficulty in progression of energy.

2. Regression of libido (depression, lack of disposable energy).

3. Activation of unconscious contents (infantile fantasies, complexes, archetypal images, inferior function, opposite attitude, shadow, anima/animus, etc.). Compensation.

4. Formation of neurotic symptoms (confusion, fear, anxiety, guilt, moods, addictions, emotional volatility, etc.).

5. Unconscious or half-conscious conflict between the ego and contents activated in the unconscious. Inner tension. Defensive reactions.

6. Activation of the transcendent function, involving the Self and archetypal patterns of wholeness (mandalas, etc.).

7. Formation of symbols (numinosity, synchronicity).

8. Transfer of energy between unconscious contents and consciousness. Enlargement of the ego, renewed progression of energy.

9. Integration of unconscious contents. Active involvement in the process of individuation.

10. A renewed zest for life, with a focus on attention to where one's energy wants to go.

9i
Psychological Aspects of the Mother Archetype
(from *The Archetypes and the Collective Unconscious,*
CW 9i; vintage 1938/1954)

The concept of the Great Mother belongs to the field of comparative religion and embraces widely varying types of mother-goddess. The concept itself is of no immediate concern to psychology, because the image of a Great Mother in this form is rarely encountered in practice, and then only under very special conditions. The symbol is obviously a derivative of the mother archetype.[104]

"Moving right along," mused Rachel.

I bowed. "Thanks to you."

Rachel bit into a piece of cinnamon toast and licked her fingers. "You who? I'm you, that's who. They are your ideas."

She picked up her book, a recent biography of Shen Li, an ancient Chinese sage.

I hung around.

Rachel looked up. "Yes?"

"Sometimes it's frustrating . . . To understand X you have to know Y. That leads to Z, which involves P. That takes you to E and M. Before you know it you're caught up in J . . . . Help!"

Rachel touched my arm. "It's okay," she said, "I'm here."

I paced the room, silent.

"There's something else?" said Rachel, fingering Shen Li.

"Well . . . why does it take so long for me to write a book?"

Rachel shrugged.

"Look at George Simenon," I said. "He churned out six books a year for ten years, some in only a few weeks! My own meager output is fifteen books in thirty years. Do the math, I'm working way below my potential."

---

[104] "On the Concept of the Archetype," *The Archetypes and the Collective Unconscious,* CW 9i, par. 148.

I presented my calculations to Rachel as follows.

"There are 168 hours in a week. You need to sleep, say, 50 hours a week. Of the remaining 118, you might spend about 20 hours a week eating, or preparing to, three times a day. That leaves 98 hours. Of these, perhaps 3 hours a day are spent in some way with loved ones; that's 21 hours a week, leaving 77 hours.

"Let's assume 8 hours a week are consumed by shopping and unforeseen distractions; allow another 4 to attend to ablutions and necessary bodily functions. Finally, then, there are 65 hours a week—almost 10 hours a day—in which to write, spit or chew gum. Even if 4 of these are spent looking at the wall or staring into space, that still leaves about 6 hours a day for actually, physically, putting down one sentence after another. Do you know how many sentences you can write in 42 hours?"

Rachel rolled her eyes and said nothing.

"I do. At an average length of 10 words, even I, a mediocre typist, can write a sentence in about 20 seconds. That's 3 a minute. In 42 hours there are 2520 minutes, enough time to write 7,560 sentences—let's say 6,000 even, allowing for breaks to refer to a dictionary or consult a thesaurus.

"The average typed page, double-spaced, has 28 sentences, which means that in *one week* I should be able to turn out just over 214 pages. That's a respectable book-length manuscript."

I sat back and smiled ruefully.

"Even if I spent three months—that's 546 hours of 6-hour writing days—polishing what I produced in a week, I figure I should be able to write 4 books a year with no sweat. In leap-years I could manage at least a few more paragraphs."

I looked at Rachel. Her head was spinning, I thought she'd turn into honey-mustard.

"What do you think of that?"

"Sounds to me like a complex," said Rachel, and threw up.

*

Most of Jung's views on the subject of mothers and daughters and sons are found in this essay, "Psychological Aspects of the Mother Archetype." First there are some general observations on the archetype, and then he discusses the different qualities, some positive and others negative, that have been associated with the mother down through the ages—the kind of images and symbolic depictions we meet in literature, mythology, folklore and so on. These images of mother are in our blood, and we are always prone to project them onto an actual woman.

The most convenient hook for these projections is usually the personal mother. The archetypal element gives her a particular authority and numinosity, a larger-than-life quality, and that's what forms the foundation for the individual mother complex, which is then modified by other significant females in a person's life.

In what follows, bear in mind that the descriptions are *models,* potential manifestations of an archetype, and as such are traits that can only loosely be ascribed to any particular woman.

According to Jung, the possible effects of the mother complex on the daughter range from an exaggeration of the feminine instincts to their pronounced inhibition. In the first case, there is an intensification of the maternal instinct. The woman's primary goal, often her only one, is childbirth. She is not interested in a career; all she wants to do is to have kids. What would such a woman's relationships look like?

In the first place, she'd probably be overprotective. Secondly, she'd likely mother the men in her life. But Jung goes rather further than that. He says:

> To her the husband is . . . of secondary importance; he is first and foremost the instrument of procreation, and she regards him merely as an object to be looked after, along with children, poor relations, cats, dogs, and household furniture.[105]

---

[105] "Psychological Aspects of the Mother Archetype," *The Archetypes and the Collective Unconscious,* CW 9i, par. 167.

Jung also says that this kind of woman tends to be unconscious of her own personality. She appears to be selfless and she identifies with those she takes care of. As a consequence she would tend to live her life in and through others:

> First she gives birth to the children, and from then on she clings to them, for without them she has no existence whatsoever. Like Demeter, she compels the gods by her stubborn persistence to grant her the right of possession over her daughter. Her Eros develops exclusively as a maternal relationship while remaining unconscious as a personal one.[106]

The most common manifestation of this appears in the unconscious wielding of power over others:

> An unconscious Eros always expresses itself as will to power. Women of this type, though continually "living for others," are, as a matter of fact, unable to make any real sacrifice. Driven by ruthless will to power and a fanatical insistence on their own maternal rights, they often succeed in annihilating not only their own personality but also the personal lives of their children.[107]

Now, the second possibility when the mother's maternal side is overemphasized is that the daughter's own mothering instincts can be inhibited or even wiped out. Then the result is an overdeveloped and overpersonalized Eros. Jung says this invariably leads to an unconscious incestuous relationship with the father and therefore, quite naturally, to jealousy of the mother.[108]

This kind of woman is unlike her mother in that she has no desire for children of her own. Her focus is on romantic adventures, the more intense the better. Jung gives her rather short shrift:

> A woman of this type loves romantic and sensational episodes for their own sake, and is interested in married men, less for themselves

---

[106] Ibid.

[107] Ibid.

[108] Jung points out that the projection of the father's anima can also play a significant role in this domestic drama. (Ibid., par. 168, note 6)

than for the fact that they are married and so give her an opportunity to wreck a marriage, that being the whole point of her manoeuvre. Once the goal is attained, her interest evaporates for lack of any maternal instinct, and then it will be someone else's turn. This type is noted for its remarkable unconsciousness.[109]

Jung suggests that her fate is to be a disturbing element in other people's relationships, a *femme fatale,* but this needn't be seen as entirely destructive. He quotes these lines from Goethe's *Faust—*

> Part of that power which would
> Ever work evil but engenders good,[110]

—implying that the conflicts she stirs up can actually be healthy for all concerned, and not least for herself. Remember, one of Jung's basic ideas is that conflict is a stimulus to consciousness.[111]

This all sounds pretty extreme, but Jung had a habit of speaking hyperbolically, to make a point.

Now, Jung goes on to describe a third type of woman, another possible result when the mother is caught up in . . . well, being a mother. The daughter might identify with her mother and then be unconscious of both her own maternal instinct and her own Eros. It would all be projected onto the mother:

> Everything which reminds her [the daughter] of motherhood, responsibility, personal relationships, and erotic demands arouses feelings of inferiority and compels her to run away—to her mother, naturally, who lives to perfection everything that seems unattainable to her daughter. As a sort of superwoman (admired involuntarily by the daughter), the mother lives out for her beforehand all that the girl might have lived for herself. She is content to cling to her mother in selfless devotion, while at the same time unconsciously striving, almost against her will, to tyrannize over her, naturally under the mask

---

[109] Ibid., par. 168.

[110] Ibid., par. 181 (from *Faust,* part 1, act 1).

[111] "The stirring up of conflict is a Luciferian virtue in the true sense of the word. Conflict engenders fire, the fire of affects and emotions, and like every other fire it has two aspects, that of combustion and that of creating light." (Ibid., par. 179)

of complete loyalty and devotion. The daughter leads a shadow-existence, often visibly sucked dry by her mother, and she prolongs her mother's life by a sort of continuous blood transfusion.[112]

As you see, there would be a strong tie to the mother, while unconsciously the daughter would yearn to be free. And there is a good possibility she'd feel her mother was holding her back, which would generate a lot of tension between them.

Such women are particularly good hooks for men's anima projections. They can seem to be anything you want. Jung expresses it like this:

Despite their shadowiness and passivity, they command a high price on the marriage market. First, they are so empty that a man is free to impute to them anything he fancies. In addition, they are so unconscious that the unconscious puts out countless invisible feelers, veritable octopus-tentacles, that suck up all masculine projections; and this pleases men enormously. All that feminine indefiniteness is the longed-for counterpart of male decisiveness and single-mindedness, which can be satisfactorily achieved only if a man can get rid of everything doubtful, ambiguous, vague, and muddled by projecting it upon some charming example of feminine innocence.[113]

All the same, it needn't turn out so badly. These women often become devoted and self-sacrificing mates. That's because even if they can get quit of their mother, they're liable to project their talents, their own unconscious gifts, onto their partner. And then, says Jung,

We have the spectacle of a totally insignificant man who seemed to have no chance whatsoever suddenly soaring as if on a magic carpet to the highest summits of achievement. *Cherchez la femme,* and you

---

[112] "The Mother Complex," *The Archetypes and the Collective Unconscious,* CW 9i, par. 169.

[113] Ibid. Jung adds a footnote here:: "This type of woman has an oddly disarming effect on her husband, but only until he discovers that the person he has married and who shares his nuptial bed is his mother-in-law." See also M. Esther Harding, *The Way of All Women,* esp. chap. 1, "All Things to All Men."

have the secret of his success. These women remind me—if I may be forgiven the impolite comparison—of hefty great bitches who turn tail before the smallest cur simply because he is a terrible male and it never occurs to them to bite him.[114]

This may give the impression that Jung was a misogynist. These wet dishrags, is that all he saw? Did he ever say anything good about women, I mean really complimentary?

Indeed he did, but first the worst.

In Jung's view, the three types I have described are linked together by a lot of intermediate stages. The most important of these is where there is an overwhelming resistance to the mother and everything she stands for. This is your real dragon lady, a man's worst nightmare, the supreme example of the negative mother complex.

> The motto of this type is: "Anything, so long as it is not like Mother! . . . This kind of daughter knows what she does *not* want, but is usually completely at sea as to what she would choose as her own fate. . . . Should she get as far as marrying, either the marriage will be used for the sole purpose of escaping from her mother, or else a diabolical fate will present her with a husband who shares all the essential traits of her mother's character. All instinctive processes meet with unexpected difficulties; either sexuality does not function properly, or the children are unwanted, or maternal duties seem unbearable, or the demands of marital life are responded to with impatience and irritation. . . . Resistance to the mother as *uterus* often manifests itself in menstrual disturbances, failure of conception, abhorrence of pregnancy, hemorrhages and excessive vomiting during pregnancy, miscarriages, and so on. The mother as *materia,* "matter," may be at the back of these women's impatience with objects, their clumsy handling of tools and crockery and bad taste in clothes.[115]

This presents a pretty nasty picture, which makes one wonder about Jung's personal relationships, about which he didn't write.

---

[114] Ibid., par. 182.
[115] Ibid., par. 170.

It is appropriate here to mention Jung's views on the effect of the mother complex on men. He writes that the two typical effects, the extremes, of the close bond between mother and son are homosexuality and Don Juanism:

> In homosexuality, the son's entire heterosexuality is tied to the mother in an unconscious form; in Don Juanism, he unconsciously seeks his mother in every woman he meets.[116]

A man's mother complex is inevitably influenced by the contrasexual complex, the anima. But to the extent that a man establishes a good working relationship with his inner woman (instead of being possessed by her), even a negative mother complex may have positive effects. Jung observes;

> [He] may have a finely differentiated Eros instead of, or in addition to, homosexuality. . . . This gives him a great capacity for friendship, which often creates ties of astonishing tenderness between men and may even rescue friendship between the sexes from the limbo of the impossible. He may have good taste and an aesthetic sense which are fostered by the presence of a feminine streak. Then he may be supremely gifted as a teacher because of his almost feminine insight and tact. He is likely to have a feeling for history, and to be conservative in the best sense and cherish the values of the past. Often he is endowed with a wealth of religious feelings . . . .
>
> In the same way, what in its negative aspect is Don Juanism can appear positively in bold and resolute manliness, ambitious striving after the highest goals, opposition to all stupidity, narrow-mindedness, injustice, and laziness, willingness to make sacrifices for what is regarded as right, sometimes bordering on heroism, perseverance, inflexibility and roughness of will; a curiosity that does not shirk even from the riddles of the universe; and finally, a revolutionary spirit which strives to put a new face upon the world.

Although the absence of a strong father figure in a man's early life may be a contributing factor, where the man's heterosexual li-

---

[116] Ibid., par. 162.

bido, his instinctive sexual energy, is captive to the mother, he cannot muster any interest in girls, or perhaps he tries but is discouraged by impotence. There is a kind of secret conspiracy between mother and son. The incest taboo usually prevents this from being acted out, but the sexual urge won't be denied, and it may very well find an outlet with other men. Of course, the man himself may be ashamed of this, though there is no good reason to be for he is not wholly in charge of his fate.

Jung's remarks are applicable to what may be deemed developmental homosexuality, a neurotic distortion of what under other circumstances would be a natural heterosexual urge. This is quite different from constitutional homosexuality, where there is an innate attraction to the same sex, not pathological or neurotic.[117]

A growing boy's path to mature manhood, psychologically speaking, is strewn with all manner of obstacles. And one of the greatest difficulties is leaving the charmed circle of childhood, where the mother answers every call, meets every need. Elsewhere Jung emphasizes this in the strongest terms, referring to the "faithless Eros" required for a man to relinquish "the first love of his life."[118]

Eros refers to our feelings and how we relate to other people. Jung associated it with the feminine principle, as the complementary opposite to masculine Logos—discrimination, structure, self-discipline, that sort of thing. In the present context Eros means the man's primal connection with his mother. Jung says:

> [The world] makes demands on the masculinity of a man, on his ardour, above all on his courage and resolution when it comes to throwing his whole being into the scales. For this he would need a faithless Eros, one capable of forgetting his mother and undergoing the pain of relinquishing the first love of his life.[119]

---

[117] "Concerning the Archetypes and the Anima Concept," ibid., par. 146.
[118] "The Syzygy: Anima and Animus," *Aion,* CW 9ii, par. 22.
[119] Ibid.

And then he pinpoints the mother's unconscious hold:

The mother, foreseeing this danger, has carefully inculcated into him the virtues of faithfulness, devotion, loyalty, so as to protect him from the moral disruption which is the risk of every life adventure. He has learnt these lessons only too well, and remains true to his mother.[120]

The possible result leads right back to the homosexual issue:

This naturally causes her the deepest anxiety (when, to her greater glory, he turns out to be a homosexual, for example) and at the same time affords her an unconscious satisfaction that is positively mythological. For, in the relationship now reigning between them, there is consummated the immemorial and most sacred archetype of the marriage of mother and son. What, after all, has commonplace reality to offer, with its registry offices, pay envelopes, and monthly rent, that could outweigh the mystic awe of the *hieros gamos?*[121]

I should say, too, that a father who is afraid of his homoerotic shadow, his attraction to other men, can also be instrumental in his son's unconscious movement in that direction.

Marie-Louise von Franz explains what is meant psychologically by "a faithless Eros":

That would mean the capacity to turn away from time to time from a relationship . . . . The *puer aeternus*, in the negative sense of the word, very often tends to be too impressed, too weak, and too much of a "good boy" in his relationships, without a quick self-defense reaction where required.[122]

To "turn away" from a relationship does not necessarily mean to leave it, or to stop loving someone. It may simply involve paying more attention to oneself than to the other person. But even this much is a heroic feat for a man with a positive mother complex. It requires a ruthlessness, or self-confidence, that is alien to his ego

---

[120] Ibid.

[121] Ibid.

[122] *The Problem of the Puer Aeternus,* p. 52.

but characteristic of his unsentimental shadow. If he is not up to it—which to someone he's involved with may look like a lack of relatedness, no heart—he will suffer the consequence: loss of soul.

Let us turn now to the less deleterious effects of the mother complex on a daughter: Jung begins this section with these words:

> The positive aspect of the first type of complex, namely the overde-velopment of the maternal instinct, is identical with that well-known image of the mother which has been glorified in all ages and all tongues. This is the mother-love which is one of the most moving and unforgettable memories of our lives, the mysterious root of all growth and change; the love that means homecoming, shelter, and the long silence from which everything begins and in which every-thing ends. Intimately known and yet strange like Nature, lovingly tender and yet cruel like fate, joyous and untiring giver of life—*mater dolorosa* and mute implacable portal that closes upon the dead.[123]

Jung expresses appreciation too for the woman with the overde-veloped Eros, the *femme fatale* who seems programmed to rattle the complacency of married men:

> This type often develops in reaction to a mother who is wholly a thrall of nature, purely instinctive and therefore all-devouring. Such a mother is an anachronism, a throw-back to a primitive state of ma-triarchy where the man leads an insipid existence as a mere procrea-tor and serf of the soil. The reactive intensification of the daughter's Eros is aimed at some man who ought to be rescued from the pre-ponderance of the female maternal element in his life. A woman of this type instinctively intervenes when provoked by the uncon-sciousness of [another woman's] marriage partner. She will disturb that comfortable ease so dangerous to the personality of a man but frequently regarded by him as marital faithfulness.[124]

This type of woman is akin to a sexual predator. She directs "the

---

[123] "Positive Aspects of the Mother Complex," *The Archetypes and the Collective Unconscious,* CW 9i, par. 172

[124] Ibid., par. 176.

burning ray of her Eros" upon a man whose life is stifled by maternal solicitude. By doing so she arouses in the man a moral conflict which we must regard in a positive light since it may in the long run lead to him becoming more conscious of his own personality. As well, she may herself become more conscious, evolving from destroyer to deliverer and redeemer.

The third type of woman, whom Jung dubs the "nothing but" daughter, is so identified with the mother that her own instincts are paralyzed. If she is fortunate, her dormant talents will be constellated by an adoring man who wrests her from her mother because he finds her "mysterious" and fills her empty vessel with a powerful anima projection, which she repays with unstinting support for his endeavors and career. She is the legendary power behind her mate's throne.

More fortunate still, and she will come to tire of her secondary role in their social charade, realizing that his success is due to the projection of her own gifts. Thus such women may become successful businesswomen in later life.

Jung ends this essay with a rather abrasive description of the woman with a powerful negative mother complex:

> This type is an unpleasant, exacting, and anything but satisfactory partner for her husband, since she rebels in every fibre of her being against everything that springs from natural soil.[125]

And yet he sees possibilities in even such a harridan, whose experience of life may over time temper her aversion to everything maternal:

> Excelling her more feminine sister in her objectivity and coolness of judgment, she may become the friend, sister, and competent advisor of her husband. Her own masculine aspirations make it possible for her to have a human understanding of the individuality of her husband quite transcending the realm of the erotic. The woman with this type of mother complex probably has the best chance of all to

---

[125] Ibid., par. 184.

make her marriage an outstanding success during the second half of life. But this is true only if she succeeds in overcoming the hell of "nothing but femininity," the chaos of the maternal womb.[126]

It is in this context that Jung makes the memorable observation that anyone aspiring to become more conscious might take to heart:

> A complex can be really overcome only if it is lived out to the full. In other words, if we are to develop further we have to draw to us and drink down to the very dregs what, because of our complexes, we have held at a distance.[127]

Be that as it may, the underside of a woman's negative mother complex may eventually manifest positively in a cool intelligence, a clarity of understanding, and the ability to function as a spiritual guide to her mate. Such a woman is not frightening to a man because she builds bridges for the masculine mind over which he can safely guide his feelings to the opposite shore. She too may manage productive organizations in later life.

Some of Jung's views on the effects of the mother complex seem quite harsh, but remember they are only models, examples of what might be, not descriptive of any particular woman. Still, many ring true according to women I have known. Jung's observations have given me a handle on my own emotional landscape, and I am grateful for that. I once would have given my all to save Mimi, consumptive heroine of *La Bohème*. Moreover, he enlightened women about themselves, as witness the works of many female Jungian analysts listed here in the bibliography.[128]

Whatever impression one may have from this essay, it is well known that Jung loved women, and they responded. At one point, the coterie of females in his thrall were known as *Jung Frau*

---

[126] Ibid.

[127] Ibid.

[128] See, for instance, Marion Woodman, Sylvia Brinton Perera, Rachel Hillel, M. Esther Harding, Emma Jung, Linda Leonard, Cara Barker and Nancy Qualls-Corbett

(Jung's women). As a matter of fact, Jung's work overall has been credited with raising the awareness of both men and women in contemporary Western culture of the importance of everything traditionally associated with the feminine principle—Eros, relatedness, feeling, intuition, etc., bringing it out of the closet, so to speak.

Perhaps Jung's most significant contribution in this area was to identify the feminine as the needed balance in a world that functions overwhelmingly according to Logos and traditional masculine values. And in that sense he was decidedly an antipatriarchal pioneer, a standard-bearer for enlightened feminism.

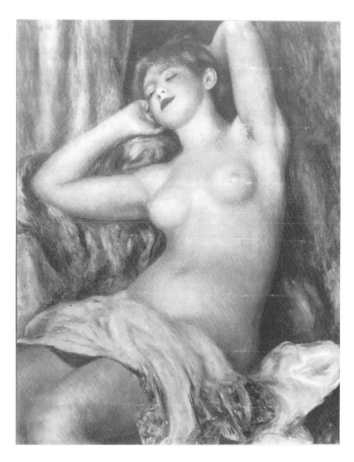

Figure 6. Sleeping Nude, by Auguste Renoir.
(Private collection, Switzerland.)

Afterword

It was not easy to choose which of Jung's essays to write about in this book. Jung's *Collected Works* are such a cornucopia. As an inveterate "classical Jungian," I believe that everything he wrote deserves close attention.

My choices, then, have been somewhat arbitrary and entirely subjective. I can only hope they find some favor with readers and stimulate them to go to the sources for further enlightenment on the significance and importance of analytical psychology today.

*

This concludes Book One of *Jung Uncorked*. Book Two, published separately, explicates and comments on passages from Jung's *Collected Works* volumes CW 9ii *(Aion)*, to CW 18 *(The Symbolic Life)*. It has its own bibliography and index.

Bibliography

Adler, Alfred. *The Individual Psychology of Alfred Adler.* Ed. Heinz Ansbacher and Rowena Ansbacher. New York: Basic Books, 1956.

Barker, Cara. *World Weary Woman: Her Wound and Transformation.* Toronto: Inner City Books, 2001.

Bulfinch, Thomas. *Bulfinch's Mythology: The Age of Fable.* Garden City, NY: Doubleday & Company, 1968.

Carotenuto, Aldo. *Eros and Pathos: Shades of Love and Suffering.* Toronto: Inner City Books, 1989.

de Vries, Ad. *Dictionary of Imagery and Symbolism.* Amsterdam: North-Holland Publishing Co., 1974.

Dostoyevsky, Fyodor. *Notes from Underground.* Trans. Andrew McAndrew. New York: Signet, 1961.

Edinger, Edward F. *The Aion Lectures: Exploring the Self in Jung's* Aion. Toronto: Inner City Books, 1996.

_____. *Encounter with the Self: A Jungian Commentary on William Blake's* Illustrations of the Book of Job. Toronto: Inner City Books, 1986.

_____. *Science of the Soul: A Jungian Perspective.* Toronto: Inner City Books, 2002.

_____. *Transformation of the God-Image: An Elucidation of Jung's "Answer to Job."* Toronto: Inner City Books, 1992.

Freud, Sigmund. *The Complete Psychological Works of Sigmund Freud.* Ed. James Strachey. London, UK: The Hogarth Press, 1978.

Frey-Rohn, Liliane. *From Freud to Jung: A Comparative Study of the Psychology of the Unconscious.* Boston: Shambhala Publications, 1974.

Grimm Brothers. *Complete Grimm's Fairy Tales.* New York: Pantheon Books, 1944.

Hannah, Barbara. *Jung: His Life and Work (A Biographical Memoir).* New York: Capricorn Books, G.P. Putnam's Sons, 1976.

Harding, M. Esther. *The Way of All Women: A Psychological Interpretation.* London, UK: Rider & Company, 1971.

_____. *Woman's Mysteries: Ancient and Modern.* New York: C.G. Jung Foundation for Analytical Psychology, 1971.

_____. *The Parental Image: Its Injury and Reconstruction.* Toronto: Inner City Books, 2003.

Hillel, Rachel. *The Redemption of the Feminine Erotic Soul.* York Beach, ME: Nicholas-Hayes, Inc., 1997.

Hillman, James. *The Force of Character and the Lasting Life.* New York: Ballantine, 1999.

_____. *Loose Ends.* Zurich: Spring Publications, 1975.

_____. *The Myth of Analysis: Three Essays in Archetypal Psychology.* Evanston, IL: Northwestern University Press, 1972.

Hollis, James. *Creating a Life: Finding Your Individual Path.* Toronto: Inner City Books, 2001.

_____. *The Middle Passage: From Misery to Meaning in Midlife.* Toronto: Inner City Books, 1993.

Jacoby, Mario. *The Analytic Encounter: Transference and Human Relationship.* Toronto: Inner City Books, 1984.

_____. *Longing for Paradise: Psychological Perspectives on an Archetype.* Toronto: Inner City Books, 2006.

Jaffe, Lawrence W. *Liberating the Heart: Spirituality and Jungian Psychology.* Toronto: Inner City Books, 1990.

Janouch, Gustav. *Conversations with Kafka.* Trans. Goronwy Rees. 2nd edition, revised and enlarged. London, UK: Andre Deutsch, 1971.

Jung, C.G. *C.G. Jung Letters.* (Bollingen Series XCV). 2 vols. Ed. Gerhard Adler and Aniela Jaffé. Princeton: Princeton University Press, 1973.

_____. *The Collected Works of C.G. Jung* (Bollingen Series XX). 20 vols. Trans. R.F.C. Hull. Ed. H. Read, M. Fordham, G. Adler, Wm. McGuire. Princeton: Princeton University Press, 1953-1979.

_____. *Memories, Dreams, Reflections.* Ed. Aniela Jaffé. New York: Pantheon Books, 1961.

Jung, Carl G., and von Franz, Marie-Louise, eds. *Man and His Symbols.* London, UK: Aldus Books, 1964.

Jung, Emma. *Animus and Anima: Two Essays.* Woodstock, CT: Spring Publications, 1985.

Kafka, Franz. *The Diaries of Franz Kafka,, 1910-1913.* Trans. Joseph Kresh. Ed. Max Brod. London, UK: Secker & Warburg, 1948.

_____. *The Diaries of Franz Kafka,, 1916-1923.* Trans. Martin Greenberg and Hannah Arendt. Ed. Max Brod. London, UK: Secker & Warburg, 1949.

_____. *The Penal Colony: Stories and Short Pieces.* Trans. Willa and Edwin Muir. New York: Schocken Books, 1961.

Leonard, Linda. *The Wounded Woman: Healing the Father-Daughter Relationship.* Boston: Shambhala Publications, 1998.

McGuire, William, ed. *The Freud/Jung Letters* (Bollingen Series XCIV). Trans. Ralph Manheim and R.F.C. Hull. Princeton: Princeton University Press, 1974.

McGuire, William, and Hull, R.F.C., eds. *C.G. Jung Speaking: Interviews and Encounters* (Bollingen Series XCVII). Princeton: Princeton University Press, 1977.

Onians, R.B. *The Origins of European Thought.* Cambridge, MA: Cambridge University Press, 1951.

Perera, Sylvia Brinton. *Descent to the Goddess: A Way of Initiation for Women.* Toronto: Inner City Books, 1981.

_____. *The Irish Bull God: Images of Multiform and Integral Masculinity.* Toronto: Inner City Books, 2004.

Qualls-Corbett, Nancy. *Awakening Woman: Dreams and Individuation.* Toronto: Inner City Books, 2002.

_____. *The Sacred Prostitute: Eternal Aspect of the Feminine.* Toronto: Inner City Books, 1988.

Rank, Otto. *The Trauma of Birth.* New York: Robert Brunner, 1952.

Shamdasani, Soni, ed. *The Psychology of Kundalini Yoga: Notes of the Seminar Given in 1932 by C.G. Jung* (Bollingen Series XCIX). Princeton: Princeton University Press, 1996.

Sharp, Daryl. *Chicken Little: The Inside Story (a Jungian romance).* Toronto: Inner City Books, 1993.

_____. *Dear Gladys: The Survival Papers, Book. 2.* Toronto: Inner City Books, 1989.

_____. *Eyes Wide Open: Late Thoughts (a Jungian romance).* Toronto: Inner City Books, 2007.

_____. *Jung Lexicon: A Primer of Terms and Concepts.* Toronto: Inner City Books, 1991.

_____. *Jungian Psychology Unplugged: My Life as an Elephant.* Toronto, Inner City Books, 1998.

_____. *Living Jung: The Good and the Better.* Toronto: Inner City Books, 1996.

_____. *Not the Big Sleep: On Having Fun, Seriously (a Jungian romance).* Toronto: Inner City Books, 2005.

_____. *On Staying Awake: Getting Older and Bolder (another Jungian romance). Toronto: Inner City Books, 2006.*

_____. *Personality Types: Jung's Model of Typology.* Toronto: Inner City Books, 1987.

_____. *The Secret Raven: Conflict and Transformation in the Life of Franz Kafka.* Toronto: Inner City Books, 1980.

_____. *The Survival Papers: Anatomy of a Midlife Crisis.* Toronto: Inner City Books, 1988.

_____. *Who Am I, Really? Personality, Soul and Individuation.* Toronto: Inner City Books, 1995.

Singer, June. *Androgyny.* London, UK: Routledge & Kegan Paul, 1977.

Sparks, J. Gary. *At the Heart of Matter: Synchronicity and Jung's Spiritual Testament.* Toronto: Inner City Books, 2007

Stevens, Anthony. *Archetype Revisited: An Updated Natural History of the Self.* Toronto: Inner City Books, 2003.

von Franz, Marie-Louise. *Alchemy: An Introduction to the Symbolism and the Psychology.* Toronto: Inner City Books, 1980.

_____. *Animus and Anima in Fairy Tales.* Toronto: Inner City Books, 2002.

_____. *C.G. Jung: His Myth in Our Time.* Toronto: Inner City Books, 1998.

_____. *The Interpretation of Fairy Tales.* Zurich: Spring Publications, 1973.

_____. *On Divination and Synchronicity.* Toronto: Inner City Books, 1980.

_____. *The Problem of the Puer Aeternus.* Toronto: Inner City Books, 2000.

_____. *A Psychological Interpretation of the Golden Ass of Apuleius: The Liberation of the Feminine in Man.* Revised ed. Boston: Shambhala Publications, 1992.

_____. *Redemption Motifs in Fairy Tales.* Toronto: Inner City Books, 1980.

Von Franz, Marie-Louise, ed. with commentary. *Aurora Consurgens: A Document Attributed to Thomas Aquinas on the Problem of Opposites in Alchemy.* Toronto: Inner City Books, 2000.

Von Franz, Marie-Louise, and Hillman, James. *Jung's Typology.* New York: Spring Publications, 1971.

Wilhelm, Richard, trans. *The I Ching or Book of Changes.* London: Routledge and Kegan Paul, 1968.

Woodman, Marion. *Addiction to Perfection: The Still Unravished Bride.* Toronto: Inner City Books, 1982

_____. *Conscious Femininity: Interviews with Marion Woodman.* Toronto: Inner City Books, 1993.

_____. *The Owl Was a Baker's Daughter: Obesity, Anorexia Nervosa and the Repressed Feminine.* Toronto: Inner City Books, 1980.

_____. *The Pregnant Virgin: A Process of Psychological Transformation.* Toronto: Inner City Books, 1985.

Index

Entries in *italics* refer to illustrations

Also by Daryl Sharp in this Series

Please see last page for discounts and postage/handling.

THE SECRET RAVEN
Conflict and Transformation in the Life of Franz Kafka
ISBN 978-0-919123-00-7. (1980) 128 pp. $25

PERSONALITY TYPES: Jung's Model of Typology
ISBN 978-0-919123-30-9. (1987) 128 pp. Diagrams $25

THE SURVIVAL PAPERS: Anatomy of a Midlife Crisis
ISBN 978-0-919123-34-2. (1988) 160 pp. $25

DEAR GLADYS: The Survival Papers, Book 2
ISBN 978-0-919123-36-6. (1989) 144 pp. $25

JUNG LEXICON: A Primer of Terms and Concepts
ISBN 978-0-919123-48-9. (1991) 160 pp. Diagrams $25

GETTING TO KNOW YOU: The Inside Out of Relationship
ISBN 978-0-919123-56-4. (1992) 128 pp. $25

THE BRILLIG TRILOGY:

1. CHICKEN LITTLE: The Inside Story *(A Jungian romance)*
ISBN 978-0-919123-62-5. (1993) 128 pp. $25

2. WHO AM I, REALLY? Personality, Soul and Individuation
ISBN 978-0-919123-68-7. (1995) 144 pp. $25

3. LIVING JUNG: The Good and the Better
ISBN 978-0-919123-73-1. (1996) 128 pp. $25

JUNGIAN PSYCHOLOGY UNPLUGGED: My Life as an Elephant
ISBN 978-0-919123-81-6. (1998) 160 pp. $25

DIGESTING JUNG: Food for the Journey
ISBN 978-0-919123-96-0. (2001) 128 pp. $25

JUNG UNCORKED: Rare Vintages from the Cellar of Analytical Psychology
Two books. ISBN 978-1-894574-21-1/22-8.. (2008) 128 pp. each. $25 each

THE SLEEPNOT TRILOGY:

1. NOT THE BIG SLEEP: On having fun, seriously *(A Jungian romance)*
ISBN 978-0-894574-13-6. (2005) 128 pp. $25

2. ON STAYING AWAKE: Getting Older and Bolder *(Another Jungian romance)*
ISBN 978-0-894574-16-7. (2006) 144 pp. $25

3. EYES WIDE OPEN: Late Thoughts *(Another Jungian romance)*
ISBN 978-0-894574-18-1.. (2007) 160 pp. $25

125

Also in this Series, by Edward F. Edinger

Also in this Series, by Marie-Louise von Franz

AURORA CONSURGENS: On the Problem of Opposites in Alchemy
ISBN 978-0-919123-90-8. (2000) 576pp. **30-page Index** *Sewn* $50
A penetrating commentary on a rare medieval treatise, scattered throughout with insights relevant to the process of individuation in modern men and women.

THE PROBLEM OF THE PUER AETERNUS
ISBN 978-0-919123-88-5. (2000) 288pp. **11 illustrations** *Sewn* $40
The term *puer aeternus* (Latin, eternal youth) is used in Jungian psychology to describe a certain type of man or woman: charming, creative, and ever in pursuit of their dreams. This is the classic study of those who remain adolescent well into their adult years.

THE CAT: A Tale of Feminine Redemption
ISBN 978-0-919123-84-7. (1999) 128pp. **8 illustrations** *Sewn* $25
"The Cat" is a Romanian fairy tale about a princess who at the age of seventeen is bewitched—turned into a cat. . . . One by one von Franz unravels the symbolic threads.

C.G. JUNG: His Myth in Our Time
ISBN 978-0-919123-78-6. (1998) 368pp. **30-page Index** *Sewn* $40
The most authoritative biography of Jung, comprising an historical account of his seminal ideas, including his views on the collective unconscious, archetypes and complexes, typology, creativity, active imagination and individuation.

ARCHETYPAL PATTERNS IN FAIRY TALES
ISBN 978-0-919123-77-9. (1997) 192pp. *Sewn* $30
In-depth studies of six fairy tales—from Spain, Denmark, China, France and Africa, and one from the Grimm collection—with references to parallel themes in many others.

REDEMPTION MOTIFS IN FAIRY TALES
ISBN 978-0-919123-01-4. (1980) 128pp. *Sewn* $25
A nonlinear approach to the significance of fairy tales for an understanding of the process of psychological development. Concise explanations of complexes, projection, archetypes and active imagination. A modern classic.

ON DIVINATION AND SYNCHRONICITY
The Psychology of Meaningful Chance
ISBN 978-0-919123-02-1. (1980) 128pp. **15 illustrations** *Sewn* $25
A penetrating study of the psychological aspects of time, number and methods of divining fate such as the I Ching, astrology, Tarot, palmistry, dice, etc. Extends and amplifies Jung's work on synchronicity, contrasting Western attitudes with those of the East.

ALCHEMY: An Introduction to the Symbolism and the Psychology
ISBN 978-0-919123-04-5. (1980) 288pp. **84 illustrations** *Sewn* $40
Designed as an introduction to Jung's weightier writings on alchemy. Invaluable for interpreting images in modern dreams and for an understanding of relationships. Rich in insights from analytic experience.

Studies in Jungian Psychology
by Jungian Analysts

Quality Paperbacks

Prices and payment in $US (except in Canada, and Visa orders, $Cdn)

Jung Uncorked: Rare Vintages from the Cellar of Analytical Psychology
Two vols.. *Daryl Sharp (Toronto)* ISBN 978-1-894574-21-1/22-8. 128 pp. $25 each

Jung and Yoga: The Psyche-Body Connection
Judith Harris (London, Ontario) ISBN 978-0-919123-95-3. 160 pp. $25

The Gambler: Romancing Lady Luck
Billye B. Currie (Jackson, MS) 978-1-894574-19-8. 128 pp. $25

Conscious Femininity: Interviews with Marion Woodman
Introduction by Marion Woodman (Toronto) ISBN 978-0-919123-59-5. 160 pp. $25

The Sacred Psyche: A Psychological Approach to the Psalms
Edward F. Edinger (Los Angeles) ISBN 978-1-894574-09-9. 160 pp. $25

Eros and Pathos: Shades of Love and Suffering
Aldo Carotenuto (Rome) ISBN 978- 0-919123-39-7. 144 pp. $25

Descent to the Goddess: A Way of Initiation for Women
Sylvia Brinton Perera (New York) ISBN 978-0-919123-05-2. 112 pp. $25

Addiction to Perfection: The Still Unravished Bride
Marion Woodman (Toronto) ISBNj 978-0-919123-11-3. Illustrated. 208 pp. $30/$35hc

The Illness That We Are: A Jungian Critique of Christianity
John P. Dourley (Ottawa) ISBN 978-0-919123-16-8. 128 pp. $25

Coming To Age: The Croning Years and Late-Life Transformation
Jane R. Prétat (Providence) ISBN 978-0-919123-63-2. 144 pp. $25

Jungian Dream Interpretation: A Handbook of Theory and Practice
James A. Hall, M.D. (Dallas) ISBN 978-0-919123-12-0. 128 pp. $25

Phallos: Sacred Image of the Masculine
Eugene Monick (Scranton) ISBN 978-0-919123-26-7. 30 illustrations. 144 pp. $25

The Sacred Prostitute: Eternal Aspect of the Feminine
Nancy Qualls-Corbett (Birmingham) ISBN 978-0-919123-31-1. Illustrated. 176 pp. $30

Longing for Paradise: Psychological Perspectives on an Archetype
Mario Jacoby (Zurich) ISBN 978-1-894574-17-4. 240 pp. $35

The Pregnant Virgin: A Process of Psychological Development
Marion Woodman (Toronto) ISBN 978-0-919123-20-5. Illustrated. 208 pp. $30pb/$35hc

Discounts: any 3-5 books, 10%; 6-9 books, 20%; 10-19, 25%; 20 or more, 40% .
Add Postage/Handling: 1-2 books, $6 surface ($10 air); 3-4 books, $8 surface
($12 air); 5-9 books, $15 surface ($20 air); 10 or more, $15 surface ($30 air)

Visa credit cards accepted. Toll-free: Tel. 1-888-927-0355; Fax 1-888=924-1814.

INNER CITY BOOKS
Box 1271, Station Q, Toronto, ON M4T 2P4, Canada

Tel. (416) 927-0355 / Fax (416) 924-1814 / booksales@innercitybooks.net